Clinical Dicta
and Contra Dicta

The Therapy Process from
Inside Out and Outside In

John E. Espy, Ph.D.

Published by Open Books

Copyright © 2019 by John E. Espy

Interior design by Siva Ram Maganti

Cover image © John E. Espy

ISBN-13: 978-1948598262

"We may travel a while together but we journey alone."

—Peter Matthiessen,
personal communication, February 1997

"Look at the stone cutter hammering away at his rock, perhaps a hundred times without so much a crack showing in it. Yet at the hundred-and-first blow it will split in two, and I know it was not the last blow that did it, but all that had gone before."

—Jacob Riis

Introduction

Clinical Dicta and Contra Dicta is a series of "thoughts" that I have pondered in one form or another over the past thirty-five years of practice. Some are more theoretically or philosophically based while the others tend to be more clinically specific. Many represent what I think of as truisms as I sit with, listen to, and be with my patients. The word patient seems to have gone out of the clinical lexicon these days, replaced by "client" or in some cases, "customer." Be that as it may, I still prefer "patient" as patient is a reference to one who is suffering. Recently I went to my attorney to draft up a will. I was not suffering when I went to see him and became his client. A few days later, I bought a new tractor. Perhaps my acreage was suffering from a lack of tractorial attention, but I was not suffering when I became a customer in its purchase. I think that in many ways the process of psychotherapy has gotten away from us. By *us* I mean clinicians. Likely it began many years ago now, when patients began relying on insurance companies to pay for therapy. Once that happened, insurance companies, as insurance does, began to look for ways to reduce their costs on one side and up their profit margins for investors on the other; hence, the rampant emergence of medications, which are now increasingly being revealed to have questionable efficacy. The most recent trend is that of pseudo qualifying or *branding* a particular type of therapy as evidence-based. By getting away from us, I think that therapy lost not only much of its humanism but it also became more plastic. Simplistic self-help books and media presentations, promising desperation-driven "solutions" are hawked by those not dissimilar from snake-oil barkers of old.

These thoughts and brief clinical scenarios that are included here are some of what I believe to be important when considering what one does as a psychotherapist/analyst. *Clinical Dicta and Contra Dicta* looks at the therapy process from both the inside out and the outside in.

Proof of this and denial of that is a fleeting concept and one must question if, whatever we conceive of proof and denial being, such absolutes have much of a place in the behavioral arts and sciences. While studying Bertrand Russell and Alfred North Whitehead's voluminous work, the *Principia Mathematica*, the mathematician Kurt Gödel had an extraordinary insight. In pondering the mass of logical statements that Russell and Whitehead had put forth, Gödel began to *imagine* that each logical operator could be assigned a unique number, and that each logical statement could be represented by a unique number formed by multiplying those unique numbers respectively. Thus he saw that the *Principia* was a book about *numbers* which used *numbers* to *prove itself*. It was, from a mathematician's point of view, an uncomfortable form of self-referential proof (a form of mathematical narcissism perhaps), which could result in inconsistencies that would raise doubts as to the *Principia's* validity. Gödel then set about to see if he could find such an example of representative of inconsistency. However, he ended up delving much deeper than this. Gödel discovered a theorem that could be stated within the confines of Russell and Whitehead's system that was *impossible to verify within* their system of proof. Outside of Russell and Whitehead's system put forth in the *Principia*, Gödel was able to prove a "logical statement" similar to, 'This formula is *unprovable* by the rules of *Principia Mathematica*.' But this "logical statement" could *still* exist within the framework of *Principia Mathematica*, therefore creating a paradox in their system corresponding to the paradox, "This statement is false." This is why Gödel is often referred to as the *cretin of mathematics*, in reference to the seventh-century BC Greek cretin, *Epimenides of Knossos,* whose paradox, "All Cretans are liars," is the literary equivalent of Gödel's destructuring of Russell and Whitehead's *eighteen hundred* page tome of proofs into two final statements:

– Any consistent axiomatic system of mathematics will contain theorems which cannot be proven.

- If all the theorems of an axiomatic system can be proven then the system is inconsistent, and thus has theorems which can be proven both true and false.

In other words, there simply is no way to defeat the system. Gödel not only demolished the basis for Russell and Whitehead's work, "that all mathematical theorems can be proven with a consistent set of axioms," he also showed that *no* such system could be contrived. And yet, we in our grandiose attempts to prove this and that within the realm of clinical theory call forth examples of *truths* to *prove* our theorems of behavior. Some we even trademark and patent.

Clinical Dicta and Contra Dicta originally began as a series of what I was calling aphorisms. Quite quickly these aphorisms became rather unwieldy to remain as what are typically considered aphoristic. Although some remain in that vein, most have gone well beyond. I cannot give an adequate description of what I have written in terms of structure: perhaps, *quasi philosophical statements of personal clinical credos*, although just *credos* may simply be most precise. Some of these clinical credos amalgamate into another. Some do not. They are written to stimulate consideration of their content. Over these many years of having the privilege of sitting with many patients and supervisees the themes represented here keep emerging in one form or another.

One of the critical dynamics that continues to intertwine itself in both treatment and supervision is that of projective identification, which emerges directly or indirectly throughout these writings. When I used to teach at university, be they medical schools or doctoral programs, the concept of projective identification was one of the most difficult for trainees to conceptualize: not to simply regurgitate the definition of the concept, but rather to see it in a way similar to how a student of theoretical mathematics sees an equation. To understand that projective identification is not static but rather free floating within the context of an ongoing therapeutic dynamic. And yet, almost inevitably when the issue of projective identification is broached it is met with either a perfunctory and rudimentary "definition" of what one imagines "it" to be or it is met with utter stupefaction.

When someone is immersed in an interpersonal dynamic rich with projective identification he or she can be soothed into a lullaby-like state of rapturous denial of either one's blissfulness or one's rage. *One* being the operationally significant word—when considered in the context of projective identification. It must ask, *who* is the original possessor of the affect being made manifest at the time? Hence we have now gone from being somewhat simplistic to a more convoluted and difficult conceptualization of projective identification.

In certain schools of family therapy, the concept of who first *owned* the feeling was recognized. Yet, it was never identified as projective identification and kept very basic in its development.

Klein first identified the basic workings of projective identification, while Bion further developed it to more of its present state of understanding. R. D. Laing cogently said, "The one person does not use the other merely as a hook to hang projections on. He/she strives to find *in* the other, or to induce the other to become, the very *embodiment* of projection." In certain clinical situations projective identification can slither between the patient and the therapist like a hungry snake looking for a quivering mouse. And it is not uncommon that the therapist knows not that they have been captured in the serpent's tightening coils until they begin expressing affect that is not necessarily unfamiliar, but is now charged in a different way. Or they begin behaving uncharacteristically, at times almost as a caricature of how they would "normally" manifest an affect, or the *introjective-identification* that has become associated with incoming projective identification.

Although I typically abhor the use of popular culture to show examples, I am assuming that *The Sopranos* has been integrated so deeply into the mainstream that it will not be fleeting or considered trite. Hence, I was intrigued to watch the psychiatrist portrayed in the show, Dr. Melfi, become prey week after week to Tony Soprano's psychic penetration, the projective identification of Tony, sociopathically titillating Dr. Melfi's unborn introjective-identified sociopathic curiosities. Week after week, she fell deeper and deeper under his spell. Week after week, experiencing her victimization, and week after week, being unable to extricate herself, until she in the final episode appears to become acutely aware of her part in his psychopathic misdeeds, only to have reached the level where her own sociopathy has been exacerbated to the point of being ego dystonic and has punctured her denial, shrouded as naiveté.

Projective identification need not be as disastrous as I have discussed up to this point. It can be comparatively more benign. Like, but again without being termed as such, and aside from serial murderers, those who know most about the dynamic of projective identification are advertisers. They want us to not only buy what they purport to be better than their competitors', they also want the consumer to be vocal in a "belief" in their product and to personify it. So not only do we feel "bad" if we do not buy it or buy a competing product, we also feel guilty. And, guilt typically either maintains a current behavior or redirects one back to a current behavior should one attempt to go too far astray. This is one of the dynamics by which sociopaths and psychopaths maintain control over their prey once they have set the hook in the lip.

In Part II there are a series of clinical vignettes while Part III takes the reader deeper into the most primitive manifestation of projective identification, that being how serial murderers utilize it to troll for, prey upon, and ultimately murder their victims. It is, unlike the first and second parts of *Clinical Dicta and Contra Dicta*, not metaphoric but straightforward and in some respects, particularly as it moves deeper into describing how the serial killer utilizes projective identification, algebraic.

Part I
Clinical Dicta and Contra Dicta

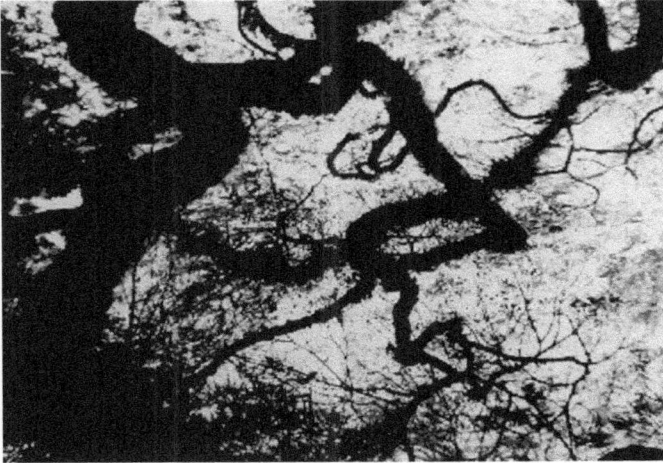

THE FEAR OF KNOWING the truth (*eo ipso*) of who we are can be so powerful that doses are lethal. What is meant by this? Truth as I think about it is being able to see, experience, and think without the intercession of illusion to buffer its repercussion(s). Repercussion, as part of its meaning, contains "percussion" which implies a reverberation or that which sets up a vibration. This is how I think of "truth." As we begin to explore this we also have to examine what we mean by "illusion." And that I would propose would be a word or diluted meaning which throws up a veil to thwart the repercussion of a truth however it is perceived by our many senses. This of course would include euphemisms and what has become collectively known as "political correctness." For example, we use the term *passed away* to mean *kind-of-dead*. Passed implies that the dead have gone elsewhere. Not that they are gone never to return or that we will, other than in our dreams or memories, never see one who has "passed" again. Away implies again a transition, which if it meant a transition from living to not living that would eliminate the illusory nature of the phrase. But the way it is used, passed away carries with it an inherent promise based upon a culturally cooperated collective heritage that the dead have moved on, like relocating from one country to another. If the kind-of-dead moved say a few hundred kilometers apart, then perhaps there would be an inherent chance that we might again casually run into them. But if the move were from country to country, the probability decreases dramatically that we would accidentally encounter one who has passed on, perhaps a kind of spiritual expat. This allows us to maintain the preconscious illusion of *hope* that, if we just keep our senses sharp, or depending upon our religious beliefs, if we have been *good* enough, we will be rewarded, upon our passing, with seeing the one for whom we grieve. The illusion of course

3

becomes more pronounced with the ego investment or love that we have for the particular kind-of-dead. A recent obituary read, "She led a good Christian life and now is being rewarded for living in the shadow of the Lord, knowing that she is eternally with her brothers and sisters enjoying her mother's pot roast." This sounds like a very long dinner.

—∞—

If the therapist is *prepared* by his own psychotherapy/analysis and clinical supervision to listen to the patient, to have his eyes, ears, senses, and intuition open, it has a profound effect upon the patient who utilizes the presence of the therapist as a conduit and medium for growth.

—∞—

Hypochondriasis is the ultimate paranoia. Once the covert physicalization of destructiveness begins to wane, the overt manifestations of destructiveness begin to be projected toward others. Once a therapist begins to understand this it immediately places him in an ethical and moral chimerical dilemma as to how far a hypochondrical patient *should* be taken in treatment if the turning of aggression against others, born out of paranoia, cannot be thwarted.

—∞—

Jealousy is a form of malignant envy.

—∞—

Therapists have to avoid becoming prey to an opioid narcissistic state of rhapsody culled from interventions that are metaphorically drugged with optimism, pessimism, or despair. These interfere with the therapist's ability to focus attention wholly on the present-centered context of the session. They are illuminations that can destroy the value of the therapist's collective capacity for seeing.

—∞—

Dialectic thought is an attempt to break through the coercion of reason and logic by its own means—not so different than Epimenides' paradox, "All Cretans are liars."

I wince when I hear a therapist say, "I *really* like this patient and *really* want to help them." I am always curious if the therapist will continue her desire to help her patient if the patient realizes how much he is liked and stops paying the therapist whom he now sees as a dear friend.

—∞—

It is more disconcerting to hear a therapist speak of his love for a patient than of his hatred of a patient.

—∞—

Calling a patient a "client" unconsciously alleviates a level of responsibility for the therapist. There appears, however, to be no ethical conflict when affixing a *client* with a *diagnosis* in order for the therapist to be paid for providing *treatment* to the patient.

—∞—

Your nine o'clock appointment is someone who reminds you that you are "not a real doctor" and that he will "go to a psychiatrist" to get a "real diagnosis" because you just don't have the training a real doctor has *and* most importantly you certainly haven't done anything for him. However, your ten o'clock patient is *wonderful* and tells you regularly of her appreciation for your great insight and wisdom. You can't wait for your nine o'clock patient to take his stale, harsh, and critical projections out the door and for your ten o'clock patient to bring into your office her fresh projections of appreciation.

—∞—

Clinical observation is concerned with neither what has happened nor what is going to happen, but with what *is* happening. For most every session there must be no history and no future—the only point of importance in any session is the unknown. This is particularly difficult for more novice or technique driven therapists. It is profoundly difficult to achieve and often arouses fear and anxiety in the therapist. However, one can also grow tremendously as a clinician from this frame of experience and perseverance. It provides for a more present-centered experience for the patient and the therapist. Those therapists who hold the erroneous belief they not only should *do* something but can do something are at risk of nullifying the therapeutic process. The unknown is a reflection of a lack of control and predictability.

—∞—

By denuding oneself of these temptations, the noise made by learning, training, past experience, and the well of unresolved conflict is (or may be) kept to a minimum. And yet paradoxically, we must have a "philosophy" by which we practice. You can immediately tell those therapists who have been able to achieve this level of listening, for they respond differently from most anyone else that you will ever meet.

—∞—

You must be able to see the almost imperceptible changes in musculature, changes in breathing, eye movement that *almost* no one else sees. This kind of observation is chilling.

—∞—

Milton Erickson knew this kind of observation. Erickson never attempted to form a cult around him. Many therapists inhibit their vision in order to maintain their alleged innocence, naiveté, and ability to cry foul when they are victimized.

—∞—

You have to be able to talk to patients at different levels of development—all with the careful use of language and inflection. Just as you have to be able to listen at different levels of development. Bion understood this and attempted to teach this throughout his life.

—∞—

A psychodynamic-oriented therapist *must* unreservedly and dangerously believe in the unconscious. He must be a fundamentalist in a belief in the power and depth of the unconscious. Most sessions will best serve the patient if there is a meeting of the therapist's and patient's unconscious. Conscious dribble for the long term serves little purpose. A therapist must be prepared to go *very very* deep, both intra – and interpersonally.

—∞—

The patient is responsible for everything, period, as is his therapist.

—∞—

The need for an awareness as to the dangerous nature of the psychotherapeutic encounter is essential. We chronically ignore the impact that our patients have on our lives. Our job is in many respects to bear our patients' madness, which must coexist beside our own. Over time this makes for increasingly strange bedfellows. Failing to be aware of truly who we are cohabitating with can lead to our demise.

—∞—

Some of the most dangerous people I have met are therapists.

—∞—

Some of the safest people I have met are therapists.

—∞—

Each new idea becomes a barrier, something difficult to penetrate; instead of being liberating, it often becomes imprisoning. Most especially when the idea becomes an ego ornament that calls forth attention to our great prowess.

—∞—

Original thinkers are confronted with the struggle of expressing new ideas and concepts in the face of opposition and hostility by those who are unwilling to suffer the turbulence involved in making a similar effort.

—∞—

When you are in the company of someone who listens ever so carefully you leave with a heightened sense of awareness and deepened perception. You walk away seeing the world with rechristened eyes.

—∞—

It is important to pay attention to moments of silence in the therapeutic encounter. If we restrict ourselves to continual verbal intercourse the therapy will slowly dissolve over time and vanish as if it were never there.

—∞—

It is possible that the murkiness of Lacan may ultimately represent the murkiness of how symbolic and imaginary constructions of the *REAL* are encoded in the human brain. Unlike most, Lacan did not censor what emerged from his unconscious with regard to how he understood language in its various forms to take shape. The integrating of Lacanian thought into developing neurophilosophy may allow us to unlock some of these mysteries.

—∞—

The faster a therapist goes, the more likely she is to run roughshod over the patient by constantly "trying to get her point across." This way the therapist can be *assured* that the patient is listening to her and her perspicacious wisdom.

—∞—

The psychic space is extremely small that exists at the margin between being consciously awake, being able to verbalize impressions, and being asleep.

—∞—

With regard to patient notes, I find them useless and irrelevant. What may have helped to elucidate my thoughts immediately after sessions, clarifies nothing at all later. I prefer to record my clinical experience into my writings, which I consider a much more valuable way of exploring the conundrums of the clinical life. I am increasingly convinced that we make notes not for our benefit or for the benefit of the patient but rather as a way of attempting to insure our innocence should someone question what we say and do with a patient. It is not uncommon for therapists to keep a separate set of notes that are reflective of their actual feelings and thoughts about the clinical work that no one, most assuredly the patient, has knowledge of. Even in a court of law it is ultimately impossible to prove their existence if one denies it. The destruction of these notes upon the death of the therapist by a trusted colleague or legal representative is essential. We are as therapists, keepers of secrets.

—∞—

Before studying the work of the original thinkers in the field of psychology consider that it is valuable to know what influences and experiences contributed to the development of who *they* are and what *they* write about.

—∞—

Read the great literature; particularly the Russian writers, who possessed a deep and profound understanding of the human psyche. From them you will discover a world of psychology far more useful than many years of therapy with an inadequately trained therapist. Chekhov, Tolstoy, Dostoevsky, and Turgenev had deep and profound insights into human relationships.

—∞—

I find it curious that alternative medicine practitioners and faith healers for example abandon their missionary zeal if they are diagnosed with a life-threatening illness, turning quickly to traditional medicine while still hawking energy-infused tinctures of snake oil to the desperate.

—∞—

In marriages or partnerships, one often throws a brick with a rose wrapped around it as a way of undermining the relationship. Then the pitcher expresses exasperation at the partner's failure to recognize the prickly fragrance of the passing petals. In an *Andy Griffith* television show of old, the character Gomer Pyle was preparing for his first date. The woman he was going on a date with was substantially overweight. As Gomer and she sit on Andy's porch, Gomer awkwardly slips his arms around the woman's shoulder. Then, Gomer looks towards her, and trying his darndest to think of something to say appropriate to the moment, leans over and says, "Gee, for a fat girl you sure don't sweat much."

—∞—

No two siblings have the same parent. Even identical twins. Fantasies of murder and sudden death of the object(s) of jealousy are commonplace and frequently induce lifelong guilt.

—∞—

It can be profoundly disturbing for identical twins to know that there is someone else who exists in their world who has knowledge of their own deep solitude. Unspoken wonderings of "Does s/he masturbate like me" or "Does s/he come like me" can plague them throughout their lives. It can also be deeply disturbing when one of the twins dies. For the remaining twin, this being akin to just having been given the diagnosis of a terminal illness, with death being not far down the road.

Antonius Block: Nothing escapes you!
Death: Nothing escapes me. No one escapes me (The Seventh Seal, 1957).

Not only is there a loss of partial-self for the surviving twin, the sword of Damocles now swings continuously above the survivor's head.

—∞—

Some patients experience a *surgical regression*, after being cut open and having their physical character armour ruptured.

—∞—

Some still seek trepanning as a means of being relieved of their demons. Is there really a cure for folly?

———∞———

Some mothers never stop resenting the child that had the audacity to cause them to be cut open just so the baby could be born. That child, throughout life, is often reminded of such selfishness.

———∞———

Faith is a personal ethos of foundational beliefs about X. Hope is a projection of X. Faith and hope can exist comfortably on parallel planes. Where things go awry is when faith and hope intersect, causing a discordance of psychic entropy.

———∞———

For growth and structural change to occur one must eliminate the projection of hope as a criterion in the initial evaluation and ongoing treatment.

———∞———

Hope is a whore.

———∞———

Hope is a study in pain.

———∞———

In psychotherapy we don't like to talk about truisms and deny they exist. If they are talked about they are "whispered" in a conspiratorial tone at cocktail parties or "presented" in scientific studies delineating the statistics supporting or denouncing the now depersonalized, anonymously research-based truism. For example, adoption. It is rare in adoptions where the child is not either extremely difficult to raise and rear or deeply disturbed. This is especially true with adoptions from other countries or other races. It is most especially true where the biological mother or father has been mentally ill or drug/alcohol involved. However, discussions of this type rapidly devolve into allegations of bias or in the most divisive cases racism or sexism. Is there a mechanism whereby we can come together and discuss our marked biases and prejudices as they emerge, process the emotions they evoke, and then move on to the discussion at hand? Imagine how much more helpful this would be to those who have to live with their truisms which are shrouded in euphemisms and conspiratorial cocktail talk.

—∞—

It does not appear that the American Psychiatric Association, in association with the pharmaceutical companies, has been able to effectively define a diagnostic category or psychopharmacological agent for treating African tribes: for example, the Maasais, whose *en masse* jumping up and down is clearly representative of a collective insanity, quite possibly hypomanic in origin but ultimately only determinable by administrating this or that anti-manic agent, to evaluate by trial and error which one most effectively quells the madness of their rhythmic surging. Opportunities also abound in third world countries and tribes just beginning to emerge from the jungles of the Amazon for newly defined diagnoses and pharmaceutical interventions. Perhaps *Spear Throwing Adjustment Disorder* would be applicable. For those natives with difficulties in successfully killing macaques, a *Hunting and Gathering Disorder* may be affixed concurrent with *Attention Deficit Disorder*, Methylphenidate may be effective in treating this disorder, increasing attentional allocation of the likely adolescent hunter, making him successful within his tribe. Should he have developed a *communal aversion* related to his *Hunting and Gathering Disorder*, Fluoxetine should be prescribed in these circumstances.

—∞—

For every therapist there is a certain type of patient he should not work with. In clinical supervision you must develop an understanding of the type of patient you shouldn't be around. Clinical supervision must be a place where the therapist can express the most dire and sexualized thoughts about a patient without fear of retribution. I have known many male residents who get erections during their OB/GYN rotations as well as many female residents who get wet during their urological rotations. And yet, their erections or wetness are rarely discussed as part of their training. Like being chronically exposed to tragedy and death, silence is conveyed by default as the best course of action in the face of the inevitable. Unfortunately over time we become impotent, dry, or dead to the life within life.

—⟡—

We teach therapeutic techniques to novice therapists as a way of allowing them to begin their work. However, the longer the therapist maintains the use of techniques as the predominant part of their practice, the more detrimental they become to their patients and stunt their own growth—ultimately acting as an impingement to resolution of inner strife rather than serving as a catalyst. Techniques also contribute to a false sense of security by caressing our anxiety and narcissism.

—⟡—

The only road map for a long-term relationship we have is our parents, regardless or possibly in spite of whether or not they remained together.

—⟡—

Lying and deceit in a relationship is the seed for interrogation while interrogation is the fertilizer for lying and deception. This is also the plinth on which politics rests.

—⟡—

The less anonymous we become the more enemies we make.

—⟡—

It is essential to confront our helplessness in the presence of both severe and mild psychopathology. Becoming syntonic with our impotence is critical to our survival.

—⟡—

The ego is the agency of the mind that performs its mental operations. It is in essence the psychic equivalent of the brain.

—⟡—

It is critical to listen *between* the words. Not just the words themselves. For example when doing a supervision session I once had a supervisee begin discussing how his patient would become "manic." I heard this as "man ick" and queried the supervisee about any possible unresolved homosexual issues in the patient. Listening closely to not only what the supervisee was saying but more importantly how he was saying it, dramatically opened up this dynamic for him. Timing is not just being "in tune," it is being able to listen to the rhythm *in-between* the notes.

———✕———

If you are a chronic victim then you have to consistently find enemies to assault you.

———✕———

Trouble raises its head when one believes that external objects can be controlled internally.

———✕———

Predators strive for immortality through their victims reliving over and over again the predator's sadism. Like a Berryman poem worming its way through the victim year after year. The victim becomes a living trophy.

———✕———

"I want to stop being promiscuous." She, being groomed to fuck her father. How could she expect to be able to call forth inhibition to put up against a stranger? She was bred to be a psychopath's mark. To seek out a psychopath's soothing lies. Her primitiveness clings to her like the bark on an oak.

———✕———

Grooming is a form of kidnapping.

———✕———

I know a therapist who screams at patients, holding the belief that they will better be able to "*get it.*" The same therapist has staked her reputation on acknowledging they have a lifetime history of lying and deception. Should we believe them? At their best, they are dedicated to presenting themselves as the consummate veteran in a lifetime of psychological warfare. At their worst, they are a psychopathic liar.

—∞—

The liar's lullaby—a sing-song timbre reminiscent of a caricatured southern drawl.

—∞—

To *fall* into love is to become aware of a longing we didn't know we had.

—∞—

For some, achieving a purple heart that says "VICTIM" is the pinnacle of their existence. To question this achievement can elicit a funda-mentalist fervor as if one is questioning the very existence of God.

—∞—

A psychopath prefers, as much as possible, to have his victims walk with him, hand in hand, toward their catastrophic destinies, as though they were in a rapturous dream carried forth by their adoration of the psychopath and the psychopath alone.

—∞—

If there is a pleasure in the "psychosis" then it is not a psychosis born out of a psychotic character whereby definition, an enormous amount of agony, terror, and internal fragmentation live.

—∞—

Unless we work very hard, throughout our lives, we become tem-plates of our mothers and fathers as we age. This is a truism that frequently engenders great denial and ire.

—∞—

Mothers will never let go as long as you continue to hang onto the apron strings. If one is treating a child with school phobia it would be clinically prudent to consider a clinging parent.

—∞—

Many children behave badly in public in order to sustain their parents' exhibitionism as "proof" of their relentless suffering.

—∞—

Plato, in *The Symposium*, spoke of God being moved by love. Perhaps this is why we need monasteries and convents to counteract church services that each and every Saturday or Sunday ask God for this and that, mostly forgiveness of real and imaginary sins. Like the little we offer to each other, we seem to offer God even less.

—∞—

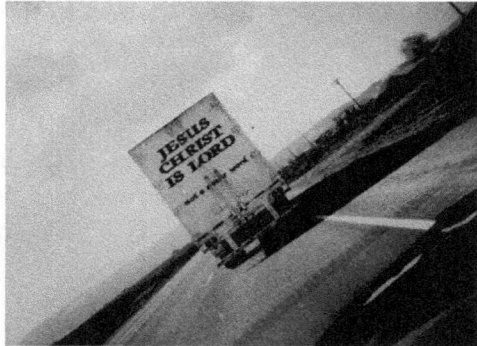

Never do we talk about how big a flop the teachings of Jesus' miracles have been. Once he ascended we no longer cure the blind, chase out the money changers, change water into wine, raise a widow's son (especially if the son was conceived out of wedlock), heal mute demon-possessed men or women, feed five thousand men and women, catch fish with coins in their mouths, or be present at a virgin conception or ascension. I wonder if Jesus is a disappointment to his father.

—∞—

People are usually more comfortable telling you how they mastur-bate than how much money they have in the bank.

—∞—

It is essential to listen to how the patient and our supervisees use words and phrases. If we believe that we hear for example a patient use a word in a particular way but the patient denies our query, do not throw out your perception and immediately become stupid. Rather, continue listening closely and see if your initial perception bears fruit. Studying the work of S. I. Hayakawa and Alfred Korzybski is invaluable.

—∞—

"All of the tension in my back is working itself out"—this state-ment is made as though there is an inner presence that is in essence *decisioning* or *considering* whether or not to leave the person's back, therefore alleviating or *choosing* to continue torturing its host. This is in contrast to the statement, "I am working out/with the tension that I feel in my back."

—∞—

What is the antithesis of dissociation? Ressociation, where one begins to *ressociate*. To begin to *re-embody* oneself as a way of psy-che reclamation. In dissociation one begins to disembody oneself in order to continue to *fend off* a *reassociation* of the memory of a traumatic event from its associated affect.

—∞—

Once you *comprehend* projective identification for what it is and how it permeates the therapeutic hours, your life as a therapist is altered.

—∞—

It is imperative in the life of the therapist to handle projective iden-tification from character-disordered patients as an infectious disease specialist would handle a highly contagious virus; to understand that psychic infections can spread just like living viruses spread.

—∞—

Some patients use transference as a psychic spell and imagine a *relationship* with the therapist that in essence represents a skeleton for creating a form of deliberation and reflection. In some respects this can be curative. However, it can also be a narcissistically gratifying experience for the therapist and ultimately become a slow-burning fuse.

—∞—

From Melanie Klein we may remember her famous interpretations of the infant child "talking" to his mother through his penis. I find this interesting from the perspective that we have to be very careful that we simply don't *make up* what we imagine our patient is thinking or feeling or how those thoughts or feelings relate to what we see as a psychic constellation. We also have to be careful not to project our own psychotic process into the hue of the transference and countertransference.

—∞—

I once heard a student say that she had "regressed" a patient, of whom she was very fond, back to the "neural tube" in order to "process" being sexually abused when her father fucked her mother during pregnancy. I asked the student why she failed to take her patient back to the moment of conception. Perhaps it would have been too overwhelming.

—∞—

Many psychoanalysts are just beginning to discover that not only patients are alive but that they are too.

—∞—

Gender is one of those things that until one lives with, fucks, or confesses to another, the nuances of being one gender or the other are ultimately blurred.

—∞—

"*But*," is the great nullifier and a window into denial. "I'd like to but ..." A man says to another man, "Yeah, Bob's a good-looking man, but, I'm *not* a homosexual or anything."

—⸎—

Be aware of exclamatory adjectives. For example, "I *really* love you." Be curious as to the origin of the affect that is sitting behind "*really*" and driving it outward. Why isn't "I love you" sufficient? What is the necessity to attempt to convince another of one's *real* feelings?

—⸎—

As long as one can "*suffer*" from, say for example, depression (or fill in the blank _____), one can wear a handicap sign and park in the disabled areas of life. One is then free of all responsibility and the ubiquitous "illness" becomes responsible for how one defines who one is.

—⸎—

Human experience can for the most part be eradicated by ingestion of psychotropic medications. In recent political protests, there was an initial ebb of outrage that quickly peaked and then just as suddenly petered out, like thousands of excited penises that couldn't maintain their hardness. This is consistent with the profound bioavailable phasing of antidepressants. There were far more sustainable penises in the 1960s as there was vastly less mass distribution of antidepressants. (The inherent sexism of this statement is not lost on the author.)

—⸎—

Politics is a study of lies and deception. A formalized mechanism where all are slight-of-mouth illusions, formulated around pre-planned denials, based upon secondary agendas. The dominant objective is not the stated "betterment of mankind," etc., but rather, the design and execution of a systematized channel for manifesting exhibitionistic narcissism. If successful, the result is unlimited power, dominance, and control. The successful construction of illusions are framed by inflammatory clichés which then become the primary lift to the ascension of power. However, ultimately the controller becomes the controlled by those whom she or he owes for providing the lift. We have yet to move beyond the master–slave dialectic.

—∞—

I know a man who, upon turning sixty, was asked by his physician if he was depressed. "No," he answered. "But you are likely to be as you get older," the physician replied. "I like to prophylactically start my older patients on an antidepressant to ward off any future depression," the physician insisted.

—∞—

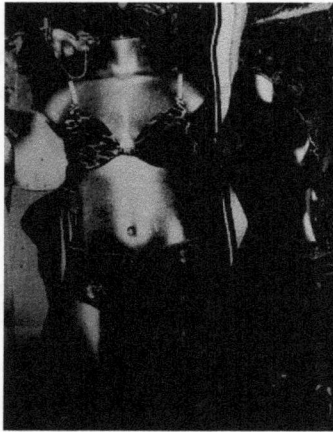

The thwarting of one's sexual nature results in resentments and rages manifested in ways that vastly "out-pervert" most perverse variations of one's sexuality. If two or more people agree to share a *perversion* does this not nullify the perversion? Homosexuality is punishable by death in countries where cannibalism is not. Is eating a dead penis considered an act of homosexuality or cannibalistic delicacy?

—∞—

When either party in an intimate relationship has to hide or suppress who they are for fear of retribution or rejection from the other the relationship has lost its vitality and is likely unrecoverable.

—∞—

Turning hostile impulses into non-feeling states and self-preoccupations eventually devolves into compulsions.

—◦✕◦—

The polarity that figures significantly in the narcissistic defense is self-hatred.

—◦✕◦—

With a narcissist you have a projective monologue by which the "self" of the narcissus is created moment-by-moment, depending upon whom they are with at the time. For this reason there is never continuity between the constantly replicating "selves."

—◦✕◦—

Psychic taffy: The quality of the relationship determines the viscosity of the bond.

—◦✕◦—

It takes *so* little of *so* little to make one feel important. Sometimes one loses one's mind with lust for meaningless power.

—◦✕◦—

It is important to listen carefully to the patient; precise work is essential. How is the patient relating to you and how are you relating to the patient? What are you experiencing when you are in the presence of the patient, before and after the hour? It is essential to understand that you are not only listening to the patient, you are listening to the patient *through* you. When you are with the patient, what do you hear inside you and whose voice resonates inside you? You may have the patient's mother, father, siblings, etc., sitting across from you and not necessarily the patient himself. You must also consider that as the patient in his various forms moves through you, he will become contaminated with your psychic residue. The more residue that litters your psyche, the more debris your image and experience of the patient will become tainted with. Hence the unalterable fact that in order to come to be a psychotherapist we must engage in our own long-term psychotherapy/analysis and clinical supervision without holding onto the illusion that we will ever be *cured* of what ails us. Rather than fixing, curing may better be understood as a way of bringing patients to a point of optimal ripeness so as to be able to function more wholly as they move throughout the spectrum of their life.

—∞—

The first two questions any prospective patient should ask of a potential therapist are: 1.) Have you been in therapy yourself and for how long? and 2.) How much clinical supervision after graduate school have you had? If the therapist replies that she has "never seen the need for being in therapy"—*run*. If she says something like, "Yes, I received supervision when I was in school; I haven't felt the need for it since then"—again, *run*.

—∞—

Interventions must be titrated with regard to the presentation of characterological material and the patient's ability to manage ascending affects.

—∞—

You must be able to tolerate the patient's chronic and long-term regression during different phases of treatment.

—∞—

The therapist must be supportive of the patient within well-defined boundaries. The boundaries need to be clearly defined so as not to further traumatize the patient. You do not want to set up an iatrogenic decompensation.

—∞—

Do not fuck, marry, or buy or sell a car to your patients. "Absurd," some may say. Really? I ask.

—∞—

Identify a present-centered process. Do not encourage visualizations early on in the treatment, particularly with those patients with a history of psychosis or dissociative states.

—∞—

Identify the individual and family character traits. This will assist in intervening prophylactically in the regressive process.

—∞—

Do not attempt to be reckless with a patient. Without proper training and clinical supervision you *can* do further harm.

—∞—

Track the titration of your interventions. Understand what is effective and what is not effective with each patient. Do not attempt to rationalize your clinical errors with comments such as, "She's just a typical borderline."

—∞—

You must be able to make yourself available to the patient. This is not meant to imply, particularly to novice therapists, that boundaries are not important. Ethical nonexploitive treatment is essential to working with any patient. Making yourself available means working with your own psychological residue and your own character issues. None of us gets out of life clean; we all have psychological histories that are replete with demons. Clinical supervision and ongoing personal therapy *cannot be emphasized enough.*

—∞—

You must possess the ability to be appropriately confrontational with your patient. This must be done with sensitivity and nonaggressively. Empathy is the anesthetic to confrontation. If you express your exasperation or anger to a patient you must do so *without* blame and without hostility.

———∞———

An initial evaluation and assessment is absolutely necessary. You must know what level of pathology you are confronted with. Do not enter treatment with a character disordered patient naively. I know of a therapist who consulted me about a patient she was seeing who was "multiple." The therapist said the patient was a national "breeder" for a quasi-religious group. But now that she is "getting older" she has outlived her usefulness and they want to be rid of her. As the therapist continued talking, she abruptly disabled her phone and said that she was sure she was being followed because she "knew" the "truth." It became apparent the therapist had in essence become part of the psychosis. However, the therapist was unable to see the severity of the patient's pathology and became increasingly paranoid, frightened, and collusive.

———∞———

You must be able to diagnose precisely, especially from a psychodynamic perspective.

———∞———

Oppositional defiant disorder is what many therapists diagnose when they have a limited understanding of obsessive-compulsive disorder. *ODD* is often *OCD* rigidity. It is not, "Johnny just being a stubborn boy." It is unfortunate, as OCD is something that *can* be *treated*.

———∞———

To be caught in an unrelenting OCD storm is like being on an unrelenting bad hallucinogenic trip.

———∞———

It can be helpful for a patient to understand that OCD is composed of "chemical thoughts."

—∞—

A little understood aspect of OCD is its boredom. There is rarely the addition of new monsters to keep the crazy-making circularity of thoughts and compulsions *interesting*. Rather it is the same old, "Am I possessed by the devil?", "Am I gay?", "Am I _____?", or "If I am _____, then this _____." A rigid 1:1 correlation exists in the mind of a person suffering from OCD.

—∞—

Individuals with character impingements must be treated long term. You have already compromised the treatment if you hold the belief that character disordered patients can be successfully treated on a short-term basis. However, such a belief may massage one's narcissism.

—∞—

Pay close attention to your own feelings, thoughts and affects, dreams and free associations. In clinical supervision or in private act out a caricature of the patient. This will allow you to experience and become more consciously aware of the patient's projective identifications that you have introjected.

—∞—

If you are unlived during the day your dreams will be unlived whenever you lapse into a sleep-filled state. Reports of "not remembering my dreams" can be a way of saying that one does not experience being alive during one's waking hours.

—∞—

All of who we are is expressed through our sexuality—*everything*. It is all there. Sexuality contains remnants of unresolved psychic conflict. Nothing, however, has been written on sexuality representing a specific form of projective identification. It is interesting that most religions promote "abstinence" or not engaging in sexual relations before marriage. However, until someone has sexual relations there is a profound aspect of who the person is that remains unseen to the other.

—∞—

Dreams *are* real. Dream reality is as real as is emotional reality. It is ludicrous to assume that simply because we are awake that we are not dreaming at any given time. Dreams are a manifestation of our representational world that brings us to a heightened intimacy with ourselves.

—∞—

Frederick Perls so cogently taught us to give voice to the *parts* of our dreams, which is how *they* live in our representational world. Perls unfortunately failed to identify them as such. In failing to do so, combined with his antics of the 1960s, he severely damaged the credibility of Gestalt therapy.

—∞—

The four losses of ego function in Gestalt therapy are projection, introjection, retroflection, and confluence. The *intra* contact boundary is that psychic space that exists between the conscious, the preconscious, and the unconscious, and those central affects that accompany the memories associated with their respective affects. *The passing of these affect states from one level of consciousness to another is what is referred to as awareness.* The resulting awareness may be accompanied by anxiety and/or depression, which serves as a clinical mechanism for the therapist to observe the externalization of the internal psychological process of the patient. This may be accomplished by the patient self-reporting such as "I am getting nervous when I talk about this …", or by the clinical observation of the therapist seeing the patient's neck beginning to flush or hearing the subtle cracking or anxiety between the patient's words. Disturbance at the *inter* contact boundary occurs between the therapist and the patient. Anxieties emerging from therapist interactions have their etiologies in both the therapist's and the patient's *intra* contact boundary disturbances. One of the requirements of the therapist is to remain aware of our own internal psychological processes: To pay attention how our own process interferes with or serves to enhance the patient's ability to successfully navigate his burgeoning awareness through the labyrinth of the UCs → PCs → Cs. Then to assist the patient in managing the associated affects that accompany the awareness. Also encapsulated within this framework is our proprioceptive awareness. The heightening of these sensations can, in certain circumstances, be used as a medium for increasing awareness.

—∞—

The loss of ego functions results in an activation of the *projective-introjective cycle*. This is the foundation of a nonorganically based neurotic and psychotic process. Introjection is an inner presence with which one experiences a continuous or intermittent dynamic relationship. Introjection is often intrusive and disruptive in its impact and psychic influence. Introjection is composed of projected psychic material (thoughts, feelings, ideas, concepts, etc.) that has not been psychologically or emotionally deconstructed. It is often perceived as having a persona-like or creature-like presence and may be experienced as exerting pressure, influence, or force over the individual's state of being or behavior independent of conscious effort to control or modify it. The primary introjects are familially borne. Once the baseline introjects are formed the external influence of the originating projective dynamic can be diminished. The influence driving the behavior is the now established internal introjective structure rather than obvious external control or free will. The originators of the introjective material now begin to create the ongoing illusion that they are being victimized by the child. In fact, they are being "victimized" by their own projections (the sprouted seeds of introjection) and are attempting to control those projections that have been laced into residence in the child. These dynamics result in *apparent* noncompliance, resistance, and *acting out* of the introjective material. Introjection is a process; it is a shift in one's psychic status. The internal representation and perception of both self and other is altered. Whatever comes in by way of perception must be filtered through the growing sticky web of introjects.

Projection is the embryonic form of introjection. It is composed of the beliefs, feelings, and affects that are interlaced into residence in another which do not belong to that individual. Inherent in the PI process are the operations of retroflection and confluence. Retroflection is the process by which a person turns the action of interaction, initially meant for the outside world, back onto the self. Retroflection, like projection, is a window to the introjective constellation. It permits the therapist to view the internal world of the patient. The therapist is able to see the areas of holding and the patterns of ongoing self-destructiveness. Retroflection is the internal reenactment of the PI process. Confluence prevents the introduction of any new or psychically challenging material. It is a state of nothingness that appears to be turbulent and tumultuous. It is also highly controlled and predictable. It is a dynamic recreated in patternistic fashion over the life span. The dynamics remain the same, only the roles ascribed to different actors momentarily in the life of the patient change. The PI process exists to keep the threat mechanism in check thus reducing the anxiety of real and perceived abandonment. Within the confines of Gestalt therapy there exists a fundamental error that has been and continues to be perpetuated by theorists and of greater consequences prevents Gestalt therapy from being understood as a model of the mind. Jean-Marie Robine (*Gestalt Journal*, Vol. XIV #1, Spring, 1991) stated, "When the id or personality functions are disturbed there is a disturbance in contact with the environment and the full development of the self is incapacitated. In particular, ego functions are suspended, unavailable, lost. They are replaced by *one* of the five boundary mechanisms (confluence, introjection, projection, retroflection, egotism)." Isadore From (*Creating Gestalt Therapy*, James Weaver, videotape transcript, p. 49, 1984) stated, "Psychotherapy, not even Gestalt Therapy, should not consist of mysteries and miracles. I would say particularly Gestalt Therapy because apparent or seeming miracles only lead to *one* of the important losses of ego function …" Consistent in the writings of Gestalt therapy is the notion that an individual develops *one* of the losses of ego function as cited by Robine and From. However, these defensive operations *do not operate mutually exclusively of each other*. Rather, *they are mutually dependent on each other*. Introjections are *internalized* projections; projections are *externalized* introjections; retroflection and confluence serve the PI dynamic. Projection relies on confluence to hold it in place *externally* while introjection relies on retroflection to hold it in place *internally*. Gestalt therapy is an organismic theory that explores the interrelatedness of the events that occur at the contact boundary that influence contact withdrawal. Failing to integrate the dynamic interplay between the loss of ego functions results in a theoretical contradiction that strikes at the core of Gestalt therapy. Examining the losses of ego function from a systemic and interdependent perspective results in a more precise method of conceptualizing the figure–ground relationships and formations including contact-boundary disturbances. A reconceptualization also permits cohesiveness in Gestalt therapy theory that has been formerly lacking. Most importantly this now lays the foundation for Gestalt therapy to be understood as a *model of the mind*.

———∞———

I am constantly looking for examples of racing thoughts combined with some type of distorted megalomania. When we think of racing thoughts we often conjure up someone who is more of a media caricature rather than what we actually see clinically. More typically we observe someone who speaks in a machine-gun-like tenor, with a pseudo authority, when upon closer listening we discover he undermines his grandiosity with woeful ignorance of the areas he claims to have authority in. As he continues to talk, his distortion, often imbued with paranoia, becomes increasingly apparent.

———∞———

Imbued within the contextual structure of the verbal contortions lives an accelerated hypervigilance or paranoia which serves to exacerbate the distortions. As the narrative continues to evolve it becomes increasingly distorted and the underlying psychotic thought process becomes increasingly apparent. In exploring this you will also be able to identify the projections that live within the introjective world of the patient. The patient will begin to appear increasingly out of control. There are however those individuals who are highly skillful at masking their underlying pathos with seemingly "accurate" *enough* facts/data/information combined with the way they present them to appear credible. This can make diagnosing true bipolar disorder more difficult at times. In addition, once someone has been duped it can become (particularly for a therapist) a narcissistic injury and result in an attempt to disprove the diagnosis even in the face of overwhelming clinical evidence. It is typically within this realm where the psychotic process is not understood by the therapist. This is frequently explained away as the patient simply "distorting" because of his "mania" rather than understanding that the psychosis is rarely very far away from *all* perceptual input and output. This is *critical* for the clinician to understand. An example is the patient who "acts" as though psychologically intact and who also coincidentally works as a therapist but lives within a deeply damaged psychotic core. The "core" psychosis of such patients is built on a ground of paranoia and perceptual distortion. They see themselves as being the interpreter of many clinical and philosophical treatises without any understanding of what they are interpreting. The unfortunate aspect, besides their own suffering, is how adept they can be at convincing others that they are not psychotic and their perceptions are *astute*. However, equally unfortunate, is the psychological debris that lies in their pathological wake.

—∞—

Conceptualizing a representational association as *"form"*[1] is more precise than as *"object."* Object lends itself to a conceptualization that whatever the representation is, it possesses some type of physical anatomy. In fact, most psyche manifestations are osmotic in their representational structure with projections flowing in and introjections flowing out with each psyche pulse.

—∞—

A projection begins when the *form*, either internal or external, provides a surface for the projection. This suggests the metaphor of the mirror. The form provides a surface that is not only *reflective* but one that is also *absorptive* (Glinnwater, personal communication, 2011).

—⊶—

It is critical to understand the fixation-frustration cycle in Asperger's patients as this frequently is one of the delimiters used in affixing a diagnosis of bipolar disorder. In the fixation-frustration cycle we observe an individual becoming fixated on an idea or a person, based upon faulty and distorted encoding of perceptive stimuli. The patient then assigns an equally faulty and distorted affect to the perception. When the expectations based upon the faulty encoding fail to materialize the individual becomes frustrated and frequently explodes with rage.

—⊶—

At its best, object-relations theory is repetitively circular. Everything comes back to the same thing and ultimately to the same kind of conclusion, either schizoid or depressed. If you read enough of the essays you will discover there is little difference between them. A repetitive rehashing of the same patient being written about over and over again, year after year. Is object relations theory a projective identification?

—⊶—

There are those patients whose narcissism dictates their coming to sessions for the sole purpose of occupying space so that others cannot. It is analogous to a child gathering up all of the toys so other children will have to go without. They so desire to contaminate the session with their presence and pathos that patients who come to sessions after them will be consumed by the vapidness of their psychic sediment.

—⊶—

People who dissociate have a familiar psychic topography. They know the geography of their vaporous inner world. And, sometimes, when all they know about how to be in their vaporous world dissolves, they find themselves in a terrestrial space that is beyond the boundaries of their *familiar* dissociative topography. When this happens they sometimes cut or burn themselves in order to return to their place of familiar and vapid dissociation. Sometimes, in your office, a gentle tapping can serve as an auditory beacon that can help someone find a sounding to navigate the way back to shore in a particularly turbulent psyche gale.

—∞—

Characterological greed frequently manifests as compulsivity. However, when the dust settles one is left perpetually unsatisfied by incomplete checkmarks beside meaningless uses of "If only I *had* ..."

—∞—

Chronic frustration and constant complaining can be experienced as more enlivening than happiness.

—∞—

Narcissism brings with it a burden. That of imagining that one is *gracing* the other's presence with one's own. This then can become a burden of responsibility when the narcissist is unable to fulfill her own projection of greatness and be sufficiently adored and admired.

—∞—

Great rage often comes from an unspoken realization of how ordinary we are.

—∞—

The narcissist also believes that he is demanded upon, via his obligation to be adored and achieve greatness. This is one of the core roots of narcissistic rage.

—∞—

A borderline personality disordered person cannot by definition repress, therefore the nonrepressed psychic material constantly spars in waking and in dream states for representation. This sets in motion ongoing chronic internal havoc.

—∞—

The diagnosis of "borderline personality disorder" is the equivalent of being diagnosed with terminal cancer of the psyche.

—∞—

Although we speak of diagnosis as entities, I have been looking all of my professional life for a 1:1 correlation of *any* psychiatric diagnosis. For example, there is a direct correlation with the X-influenza virus that causes the X-type of flu. I have yet to find a _____ that causes schizophrenia or a _____ that *causes* depression or most certainly a _____ that *causes* a personality disorder. Yet we now speak of these *diagnostic* entities as "I *have* _____." This alleviates any responsibility or association with *cause and effect* and the sufferer is free to earn others' pity.

—∞—

What has become of diagnosing? It seems to have disappeared as a clinical art form. There now are hundreds of *psychiatric* diagnoses. And, one must endeavor to understand how psychiatry, as a discipline, became the self-appointed determiner as to how we label disruptions of our mental life. *Is* attention deficit disorder really of epidemic proportions? And, of course, one must consider how virtually any suffering or grieving becomes a psychiatric malady that requires some form of medication to alleviate what are now called symptoms. It would seem that people populating the industrial nations are maladies of dysfunction who have either been given their diagnosis or have yet to be found by their diagnosis. It would also seem that as the nonindustrialized become increasingly industrialized or *civilized*, that a diagnosis will also seek them out to delineate their social stratification. I anticipate that this will require many hundreds of newly determined diagnoses. If free will is a type of causality, as Kant would suggest, then will would *only* be considered free or one could say representative of an act of causality, without it being caused to act or be determined by something other than itself.

—∞—

In the beginning was madness. Madness in all forms and curing madness was a collective rationalization for developing sophisticated forms of torture, most especially directed at women. In January, 1692, two girls, ages nine and eleven, began having fits: uncontrolled flailing and screaming nonsense. *Clearly* these were signs of demonic possession. Dr. William Griggs assessed their condition and diagnosed them with "bewitchment." The possessed girls were brought before a local magistrate and, unable to get the girls to renounce the devil, the only course of "treatment" was to hang them. Like Dr. Griggs, we continue to conjure up psychiatric diagnoses for conditions we invent. And, although hanging has gone out of vogue as a treatment for these conditions, as with say "caffeine related disorder," many of the medications historically and currently used result in a deadening of their recipient. Obviously this is not a new revelation. Psychiatric naysayers have been putting forth these allegations for decades. And yet there has been no decline in either the continued creation of new psychiatric disorders or in society's demand for medications or "treatments" that will continue to nullify our symptoms of demonic possession. Finding a cure for witchcraft still eludes us to this day.

—⚬⚬⚬—

I once knew a young man. His parents were never able to move beyond their convictions that dependency and incapacitation were superior to independence and capability, thereby setting him on a very smartly tailored path to failure and disability. He has, however, excelled in creating a pattern of disability that no one can success-fully figure out and therefore "treat." His mother and father are bearing the weight of this catastrophe successfully by finding him the best that public assistance can buy.

—⚬⚬⚬—

It is verboten to speak of patients being psychologically terminal.

—⚬⚬⚬—

"You know," often is an attempt to solicit/elicit cooperation and to reduce the likelihood of a perceived threat as well as an attempt to establish a fused schema.

—∞—

Projections are often couched as an interrogative. They can appeal to one's collusive desire to be taken advantage of. It is often important to ask, *What part of what you are saying do you want me to believe, what I hear or what I see?*

—∞—

Most unsolicited "advice" or "correcting" is an attempt at one-upmanship.

—∞—

Some say, "I got *my* heart attack on ..." or "I got *my* cancer on ..." like *it* is an excommunicated relative that inevitably returns to the fold to cause misery and suffering. Or a package we have been expecting (or longing for). Then, if God sees fit, we are blessed with a miracle, if not, then the *mystery* is invoked and our finality remains forever unexplained.

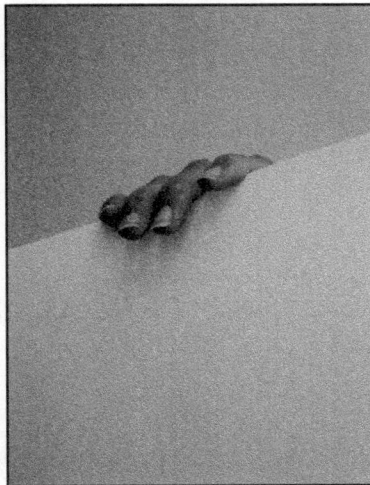

—∞—

Is God's retribution against a nonbeliever narcissistic rage?

———◦✕◦———

Grace and spiritual transcendence may be a nullification of anxiety. We then look for a systematic explanation to continue to dilute any emerging anxiety about any emerging anxiety. Little provides greater anxiety nullification than a promise of unmitigated forgiveness for our lifetime of sin.

———◦✕◦———

"*Fore*"-giveness is an attempt to use denial to send the agony that clings to the dastardly deeds we have committed as far away as possible. However, it is inevitable that someone in its path will be struck by the denial.

———◦✕◦———

For some, the lure of being probed by attentive doctors, trying to discover the cause of our imaginary ills, is too much to resist.

———◦✕◦———

Anxiety may not only be the cause of cancer, but *the* cancer.

———◦✕◦———

Fear itself has an object with which to identify, anxiety on the other hand has a "*what if*" fantasy. Fear has a well-delineated form whereas anxiety has an amorphous and ever expanding form, as each *what if* scenario gets played out over and over again in the mind.

———◦✕◦———

Malignant animosity can enter our psychic cells and consume us over time as we steadfastly refuse to grieve. Often times grieving simply for being human.

———◦✕◦———

How *much* can we proclaim that the world is run by mysterious powers before we are deemed insane?

———◦✕◦———

Transference in time is attempting to talk about the past without projecting onto the past my present projections.

—∞—

Psychic time and chronological time are different. It is important to understand this, especially within the context of therapy sessions. A session may in fact last only for the time that a critical word or phrase has found its way into the unconscious.

—∞—

I project onto you my imago of my father—but I internalize his projections onto me. My father's projection of his projection of his father's projections of his father's projections ... Who are we am I?

—∞—

As soon as "trauma" is introduced into the clinical equation, a countertransference crusade begins. This frequently escalates into the patient winning an affective purple heart for showing such bravery in the heat of battle while the therapist competes for the patient's purple heart by demonstrating bravery in a willingness to suffer along with the patient.

—∞—

In terms of our own demise, we all choose our poison.

—∞—

The efficacy of treatment is directly dependent upon the psychological growth of the therapist.

—∞—

One can reach a point in personal pain where someone no longer wants to hear himself.

—∞—

At times, ending a session early can be experienced as putting a patient out of his misery. A kind of temporary psychic euthanasia.

Conversely, ending a session early can be experienced by the therapist as ecstasy.

———∞———

Ultimately, why burden a patient with his calling to cancel a session? Just because he shows up doesn't mean he is necessarily any more present than if he were physically there or not. If, however, he shows for the appointment, it is more narcissistically gratifying.

———∞———

For some patients, "breaking down" is an end in itself. All too often, this is a hysteric demand that the therapist desperately tries to meet.

———∞———

There is no recipe for resolving grief. *All* grief is idiosyncratic.

———∞———

A few years after being in a plane crash that killed his tyrannical father, a patient said to me, "It took me almost three months before I could remember your face. Now I can see you when I'm not in your office."

———∞———

Sometimes, it helps to give a picture of you to patients with a slippery self.

———∞———

Mother-infant intersubjectivity primes and inculcates the offspring and lays a foundation for the structural development of the infant's character/logic patterns. This is a result of the mother's incalculable interactions with the child, including, in severe pathological scenarios, gaining supremacy over the child's dream world. Dominant "correctional experiences" are often necessary when the infant "veers off course."

—◦∞◦—

If we don't have a geographic "cross-pollination" of clinical ideas and understanding we become clinically *ecocentric* which devolves into narcissistic-geocentrism, imagining that *we* possess *the* defining psychological characteristics of what is and what is not. *Is* and *not* being an all-encompassing schema of that which is acceptable and that which is considered aberrant.

—◦∞◦—

The more that is defined as aberrant the more that we limit ourselves and drive those thoughts and behaviors to underground chambers of abhorrence.

—◦∞◦—

Chronic early memory problems and absentmindedness are often the foothills of dementia. But it is often too painful to imagine so we deny it. Another example of how we value illusion and fantasies of hope over what is.

—◦∞◦—

It is interesting that we diagnose children with terminal medical conditions but we behave as though there are no terminal psychological conditions. Some children, for example, are already intractable psychopaths and there is nothing that can be done.

—◦∞◦—

Programs for sexual offenders are statistically touted for their success rates but the clinicians in charge of the programs never say whether or not they would let program participants babysit their own children. I think this should be the key discharge criteria and not an arbitrary number on a checklist or the outcome of a psychological test battery.

—∞—

Some people engage in suicide on the installment plan.

—∞—

There should be one punishment for one crime.

—∞—

With psychotherapy our lives don't necessarily get any easier but often do get better.

—∞—

I have a patient who recently tried to have the Devil exorcised from her six-year-old son. It didn't work, he is still possessed.

—∞—

_A_Affectiveness is frequently misunderstood as depression. This is a little discussed phenomenon and is a hallmark of personality disorders. In personality disorders, affective neutrality must be maintained for psychic homeostasis; ascending or descending of affect is intolerable.

—∞—

Some people are _positive-affect_ intolerant. This is problematic when a therapist tries to make _them feel better_, because the therapist cannot tolerate the patient's necessary dedication to bleakness and psyche voids.

—∞—

One of the revelations of adulthood is to discover not only how much aliveness we can tolerate but for how long. This is directly proportional to how much control we can give up and for how long.

—∞—

I often wonder what it would be like for someone to come into my office and say, "I am so happy and satisfied with my life," and not be insane. We give such an esteemed place to suffering, as though suffering and suffering alone brings about great wisdom. I think though that suffering fails in its promise to do anyone any good and many people die as miserably as they lived. In all of the many psychiatric diagnoses, there is not one for satisfaction or happiness.

—∞—

It is unfortunate that we consider failure, a failure, rather than a part of life.

—∞—

Heroically attempting to break up a fused mother and child can be the equivalent of traumatic psychic amputation and can devolve into a suicidal or homicidal tapestry of two desperate homeless psyches.

—∞—

Many secret fantasies involve being consumed by an unattainable intimacy; a moving closer and closer, and, at each juncture another defense is diffused until there are none left and two become one.

—∞—

I once knew someone who was revered by others in his community for his wisdom and insight. His wife, however, would stomp her feet and slam her fists into the wall at her frustration with him for his unwillingness to compromise in any way due to his infallibility.

—∞—

People only remain normal until we become familiar with them, then each person's proclivities become fruit of the loon fodder.

—∞—

It is a mistake to define relationships as what does or doesn't dangle between one's legs. Relationships are gender fluid, each partner loving or resenting the anima or animus of the other at any point in time. Some homosexual relationships are more heterosexual than many seemingly obvious heterosexual relationships and vice versa.

—⚭—

Affairs are diversions and are usually unconsciously decided among the parties as to who will make the transgression.

—⚭—

Some confessions are good for the soul. Not all confessions are good for the survivability of a relationship.

—⚭—

When a therapist loses the ability to be surprised she should retire.

—⚭—

"Technique, technique." Who's got *the* technique? So much psychotherapy training is focused on the newest and *bestest* (and *trade-markable*) technique: that technique which is going to change our patients whether they want to be changed or not. So little attention is now paid to the development of the psychotherapist or of psychotherapy becoming a way of life rather than an extension of our own neurosis or psychosis.

—⚭—

Not infrequently, what follows when a patient asks a question is his prospective answer. However, it is difficult to wait and listen to him answer his own question when the narcissism of *our* answer is demanding recognition.

—⚭—

Neurosis and hysteria are rarely heard from any more. It is as though they left for Canada and are awaiting a pardon to return.

—⚭—

We used to be able to psychically kill our partner or family members by dropping them off at the state hospital and having them declared insane. This form of murder became financially prohibitive. Now it is more economically viable to begin deconstructing children's souls with psychotropic medications, eliminating the need for lifetime warehousing.

—∞—

For a therapist to say, "I don't understand projective identification" is akin to a physician saying, "I don't understand the germ theory of disease."

—∞—

Through the social genes of projective identification, pathological caregivers of one generation project their primitive psychopathology into their children, making them the carriers of a deadening psychological cancer. This becomes a binding legacy that crosses many generational lines. The children can experience a great sense of failure should they not be at least as crazy as the parent or grandparent they are consigned to replicate. Once the children begin producing pathology consistently respective of their parents, the grandparent(s) can then take possession of the grandchildren and raise them under the auspice of saving them from their damaged parent. Given that the grandparents have a lifelong psychological cistern for the projections in *their* children, the grandchild may fare better in a more pathologically neutralized environment. There will, however, always remain a disruption in the parental bonds which will yield an ongoing and ultimately unresolvable resentment.

—∞—

A therapist must be open to her own experience during sessions. For example, one might find oneself free associating to a patient's free associations without there being any obvious associations. The therapist's free associations may be filled with elves and trolls while the patient is free associating about a large family dinner. Particularly for a therapist of rigid thought these associations may be disturbing; however, for one who understands metaphors within the context of allowing the mind to *wander* during encounters with patients, regardless of what emerges, then one can bring to bear a new vision of the patient's free associations or description of a troubling event without censoring either what is coming in from the patient or what is emerging from within the therapist.

—∞—

When the *clinical hour* became a "unit" to be measured, it effectively murdered the *clinical* within the context of the *hour*. What was left was something to be filled for purposes of securing more funding, to justify the existence of a "program" or to meet the requirements of a secondary payer.

—∞—

Psychiatric warehousing has not vanished, rather it has become privatized and exclusive, only providing the very best in guilt-free *placements* (the benign word for warehousing) for husbands, wives, children, uncles or aunts, grannies and granddads, who become embarrassments for the family. For those without means, we now just turn them out onto the streets.

—∞—

The willingness to fervently become victimized by politicians espousing selflessness and promises of a fresh cookie in every jar represents a culture's desire to be duped by illusions that feed on anxieties of differences. We embrace psychopathic political semantics as a way of tempering our own responsibility for self-flagellation.

—∞—

Let *any* man be forewarned who tries to take away our means of artificially altering our consciousness. With these Faustian bargains we allow our ability to reason to be robbed and our response ability to be sucked out of our heads, like quelling a beehive with smoke to take its nectar.

—∞—

Proof of everlasting life, but not necessarily heaven, comes with children who become their parents upon their parent's death. "… *in my Father's house are many rooms. If it were not so, would I have told you that I go to prepare a place for you? And if I go and prepare a place for you, I will come again and will take you to myself, that where I am you may be also"* (John, 14:1–3).

—⊶—

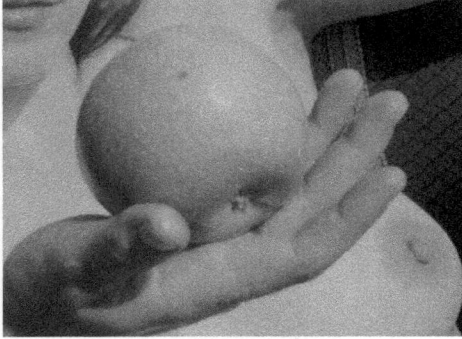

I wonder what Adam's first fantasy was. Eve's breasts or the apple?

—⊶—

I have become convinced that man, from an evolutionary standpoint, is not yet ready for happiness.

—⊶—

Just as we begin to get an idea of what this is all about we die.

—⊶—

Evidence-based credence to the aforestated cannot be claimed. It is suspected they have or will fail every test of statistical relevancy.

Part II

Vignettes

THE NON-FAMOUS SON OF a famous father enters my office. His head cocked back looking at me from aside, he reaches out with the allegedly welcoming gesture of a handshake. His hand thrusts like a harpoon. My hand intersects his, stopping its momentum. He says his name, immediately invoking his pedigree. Sitting now, he twists slightly off center making him have to peer at me over his shoulder. As he begins to speak, his cultured paranoia reveals itself to be bound in a suffering narcissism. His salvation and burden, his father. His suffering icon, his mother. His competitive nemesis, his siblings. He *whispers* his resentment of his father to ensure that he is unable to hear himself. His greatest frustration is continually wearing out mirrors and paradoxically, in his projective monologue, only having himself to live with. "By now that blessed mirror was delighting in its own inner words; I, tasting mine, was tempering the bitter with the sweet" (*Dante*, Canto XVIII).

—∞—

A young woman calls for an appointment. She is having trouble with her parents, she says. They are locking up the refrigerator with chains so she can't eat. Her father is a judge and should know better but he doesn't. Her mother is unreasonable. My caller is a woman too and should be able to do what she wants. Later that week, I look down the hallway and this young woman, who appears to be the twin of a well-known actress, is walking towards my office. She is tall, perfectly quaffed, and carries herself well-finished. She introduces herself and extends her hand. She comes into my office and begins to tell me of the difficulties that she is having with her parents. She is twenty-four, she says; there is no reason to treat her that way. She also says that in fact, the actress that she looks like is her idol, glamorous, perfect. As she relates her woes, her words are delivered deliberately, stiffly, "father" is not father, rather it is "*fat-her*". Every word is separated somewhere, not necessarily by syllable junctures but where she believes it should be broken, especially when she is applying emphasis. As she begins to perceive my empathy to her troubles, her words become increasingly disjointed and less fluent. Her anxiety begins to turn to barely contained rage. I then ask if she has ever been hit in the head, particularly when she was younger. "Yes," she says, "funny you should ask." When she was seven she was struck by a bus in Holland that came onto the sidewalk, struck her, and ran over her mother, breaking both legs. "It knocked me right out of my mother's hand, and I was stuck to the front of the bus." She would eat uncontrollably in the middle of the night. Mostly because of her beauty and ability to carry herself in a refined manner, she was able to get jobs where, for a short time, she was an ornament for the company. However, things would go awry quickly when she would suddenly become enraged and smack customers in the face or curse them for failing to recognize how good a job she was doing or for failing to compliment her on her beauty. One afternoon the hospital called. She had been dropped off at the front door. Well, not exactly, "dropped off." She had actually been kicked out of a car in front of the emergency room. She had just gotten off a bus, when a man pulled over in a very appealing car and asked her if she'd like to fuck. She didn't know him but thinking it was a good idea, without any other considerations she jumped in the car. The local hospital parking garage was but around the corner. There he drove to the top of the garage. She pulled off her underwear and he pulled out his penis and she, as best one can do in a car, shoved his penis into her whereby she immediately began screaming and hitting this unknown man on and about the head. She had inserted a tampon an hour or so earlier. When she put the unknown man's penis inside of her, he rammed the tampon deep into her cervix. He threw her into the passenger seat, and drove manically around the turnstile, pulled up in front of the ER and shoved her out the door. She lived at home until her parents died, living a life of bewildered tribulations. Her one sibling wanted nothing to do with her so she tried to make it on her own, remaining in her deceased parents' home, now having full access to the refrigerator. A few years after her parents died, she was found dead. Apparently she had been beaten to death by someone whom she had just met. She invited him in; he killed her.

—∞—

Many years ago I had a patient who at one point in her life ran a rest home for the aged and infirm. One afternoon she came home from running errands to find her husband, "a crazy man," she would say, choking one of the comatose residents. She, my patient, happened to have a revolver in her bag, whereupon she yelled for him to stop and equally upon his refusal and her concern that the comatose patient would die, promptly shot her husband six times in his chest, killing him, somewhere between one and six times instantly. She was not charged as there were finger marks around the resident's neck and of course the resident was comatose. When asked if her husband was *really* choking the resident, she would only cock her head and say how much he had beat her in the past and at long last those days were over. She also had very large breasts from which, and in particular her left breast, she would pull the nipples out with a pair of pliers and separate her breast to the breastbone with surgical scissors. She would then present herself at the hospital and say coyly that she had had an accident. One afternoon she took off her jacket and presented her left arm, where she had cut a ten-inch gash reaching down to the tendons. Her inner forearm lay splayed open and, being of substantial size, the fat in her arm was even visible. She'd tired of cutting her breast, she said. It was also one of those rare occasions where she asked to be hospitalized. Upon getting to the inpatient side of the facility, it was necessary to have her stitched up by a house physician. My patient lay in a treatment room, her wound being tended to by a nurse. A while later a very young, fresh-faced intern arrived with suture kit in hand. She walked in and saw the gaping wound. "Goodness, goodness," she said, "did we have an accident?" The intern opened her suture kit and pulled out a long thin syringe with a tiny needle. She then leaned over my patient's oozing arm and said, "You're going to feel a little stick …" My patient's mood elevated so much with the laughter caused by the absurdity that after the intern stitched her up she decided that hospitalization was unnecessary. The patient's father had left a sizeable estate. The only caveat was that neither my patient nor her mother could touch the estate's money unless the other agreed, and they hated each other. On another occasion, my patient was suicidal and was hospitalized. The following day the patient's mother and Reverend Black, her pastor, showed up at the hospital. In hand was a legal document that the mother had had her attorney quickly draft up, whereby my patient upon signing would relinquish all claims to any part, *forever and always* of her father's estate. The mother, being comforted by Rev. Black, looked into my patient's eyes and said, "Honey, since you're going to kill yourself, go ahead and sign this for your momma. It'll lessen my sufferin' after you're dead." My patient didn't sign. But she did come to the conclusion that she had to find another means of financial security. Not long after the patient was discharged, she met the man of her dreams. Her "true love of true loves" as she would say. She was forty-five and he was thirty-five, four hundred pounds, already had two myocardial infarctions and was a brittle diabetic with rapidly cycling insulin levels. They were married after a month-long courtship, both realizing the depths of their love and devotion to the other. He proved his by transferring the beneficiary from his now deceased mother to my patient and she proved her tireless devotion, day in and day out, getting up before dawn, each and every morning awaking him with the wafting aromas of all the eggs, sausage, bacon, homemade biscuits with melted butter and thick strawberry jam that he could eat, which was considerable. My patient only had to demonstrate her devotedness for three months. The love of her life had a massive coronary, finishing one of my patient's memorable meals.

—∞—

I knew of an Indian couple. He was a cardiologist and she an anesthesiologist. Theirs had been an arranged marriage. He sat on my couch and said in a heavy Hindi accent, "She does not vant to have sex with me, vix her, thank you," and upon that declaration he walked out the door. Over the next six months she discovered her clitoris and began saying to him, "I vant you to vuck me, *now!*" Not long after the announcement of her declaration, he called in a panic desperate to be treated for his impotence.

—∞—

Depending upon who "groomed" you to be a victim will determine who you choose as future perpetrators. The closer (parent, etc.) the groomer, the more impaired your ability to "see" the perpetrator in others. For example, a biological father who grooms his daughter at age thirteen to become his "lover" and tells her the world will not approve of their "loving" each other will set forth a likely intractable pattern of the girl continuing to invite others to abuse her as a grown woman. This, for her, will be ego syntonic. For her, love will seem impossible and the psychotherapeutic expedition that seeks to find her ability to be loved must be negotiated with her internalized father who continues to hold her hostage. What can look like gender and sexual issues are in reality dilemmas of bonding and misplaced loyalty. Her ability to be loved is what Ferenczi called "spellbound." She is trapped in a collective psychic desert. Her conflicted desire to be herself is met in an ongoing duel with her reality that lies in her collective heritage and her reality beyond her collective heritage. Here within this conflict lie perverted fantasies of what she imagines freedom to be, all-consuming guilt, and a paralyzed response-ability to break the shackles of her collective heritage. She speaks confusingly of her father, who she identifies as part of her collective heritage as her boyfriend, and when her jealousy of his wife emerges, she calls him her husband. "I *always* loved his body, and now *she* has it all, everything …" She sees herself as the poor suffering brute, permanently marked, scared and damaged, ultimately "un love able." Her father left his *mark* on her as he leaves his mark on everyone "'who becomes close to me,' *he* says. 'Otherwise I kick them out of my life.' My father is one of the greatest tattoo artists in the world," she says. He revealed to her that on everyone he "inks," he tats a hidden image or word "that only I can see," he said, smoking a cigarette with his naked fifteen-year-old daughter, after an afternoon of sex before his wife came home.

"It is my way of never being forgotten. They will *always* carry part of me with them." He began tattooing her when she was thirteen: he wanted to wait until she became a teenager, he said. She carries on her back the back of the head of an inked winged falcon, rising up from between her shoulder blades. Emerging from between her breasts is the sharp beak of the bird, its mouth open, looking for prey, she says. There is no opportunity for Oedipal resolution—her dreams are plagued with betrayal and loss of self. Her day residue is not a twenty-four hour day; for her time is amorphous and not continuous. Sleep-like wakefulness is a quasi-hallucination—the land of the unreal. Her massive midriff has a liquid-like appearance and moves seemingly on its own, as though it is its own life force; parasitic to its host. A toxic psychic ecosystem.

—∞—

A young boy of six was brought to me because he was "out of control" and "constantly trying to kill the cat." The boy was a smallish blond child who had deep-set, distant eyes that vibrated from side to side seeking nothing. His mother, a British civil engineer, who had spent time in the Middle East building a better tomorrow, appeared to have nothing in her prenatal history that would explain the boy's odd behaviors. In fact, an extensive month by month clinical assessment that attempted to elicit some clue as to what might have a cause and effect correlation to the child's behavioral decompensation over time revealed nothing. The appointment was during the summer and the office window was open. As the appointment was drawing to a close a bus went by, the diesel engine loudly whining as it was cranked through its gears. As the bus passed below, the boy, who had been sitting sedate on the couch, leapt up and ran toward the window, put his head close to the screen, and attempted to suck in a deep breath. I asked the mother what his behavior was about. She said, "Oh he *loves* the smell of exhaust fumes." Enquiring further, I asked her how he had ever come to "*love* the smell of exhaust." "Oh," she said, "he couldn't get enough of it from the time he could walk. Whenever I'd warm up the car in the mornings he'd plop himself down right behind the tailpipe and sit there and breathe in the exhaust." "How long did this go on for?" I queried. "Well, I mean, forever," she said. "He loves the smell of the exhaust coming out of the car, so just about every day since he was a little boy." "Does he like any other kinds of smells?" I asked. "Just the fumes of the gas when I put petrol in the car. He *loves* to stick his nose about as close as he can get to the gas tank." A few weeks later a NeuroSPECT revealed the unfortunate child had suffered "…irreversible diffuse cortical hypoperfusion from massive carbon monoxide exposure."

———∞———

I remember a therapist calling me asking for a consultation with a schizophrenic patient he was seeing. He, a handsome man, well spoken, with cold eyes. She, dumpy, disheveled, obviously hallucinated and paranoid. He begins by articulating her brokenness in textbook terms. She sits like a lump, at times swatting something I could not see. And then, she speaks and says, "But you don't like the way I fold your underwear." His eyes look at me sideways as though we are brothers in arms, united against her flagrant primitiveness dirtying our psyches. I, breaking our illusory bond, ask her how *he* likes his underwear folded. She says, "Like he likes his house cleaned, particular." "You are clearly crazy, you know," I say to her. She nods in agreement. "But," I go on to say, now turning to him, "she doesn't sound crazy about how you like your underwear tended too." He then acknowledges that three times a week she came to wash his clothes and clean his house. "Does he pay you?" I ask "No, it's part of my treatment," she says. I tell her to get as far away from him as possible before he kills her. He, now furious at my failing to provide adequate clinical supervision, storms out of my office. Like her, I too failed to please him.

———∞———

Now, many years ago, a father called, "My sixteen-year-old son is being discharged from the hospital, after being inside for six weeks. Can you see him for follow-up?" "Why was he put in hospital?" I query. "He had a nervous breakdown and began having delusions that I was a homosexual," he says. I agree to see the clearly disturbed young man. Days later, a teenager in army fatigues marches into my office and promptly pulls a knife. "What the fuck you goin' do if I cut you with this?" he asks. "I have two rules and only two," I say. "One, you don't fuck with me and two, you don't fuck with my office." Further, "Should you even try to get off of that couch with that knife, I will kick you square in the face, take the knife and shove it right up your ass. Do we understand each other?" To which he promptly folds the knife up and slides it back into his pocket. He says he was held down in the hospital and given drugs, restrained and locked in a room for days on end. He wasn't crazy, he insisted. Six weeks later, I asked the father to come see me. He was anxious for my report on how effective I was in treating his son's madness. "Funny," I say to him. "He actually doesn't seem mad to me at all. Pissed yes, mad no." "Okay," the father screamed while pounding the arms of the chair. "So some of his friends got goddam blow jobs, what's the fucking harm in that, they didn't complain. You don't understand the position I'm in being a teacher."

—∞—

James, a medical/hospice social worker, struggles with episodic psychoses and narcissistic regression. These episodes are consistently brought about by perceived threats of abandonment. James graduated with his master's degree and has been employed for several years. His psychotic process typically takes the form of increasing paranoia and perceptual hypervigilance resulting in significant cueing distortions. This results in deep misinterpretations and confabulations of interpersonal interactions, including his interactions with patients. For example during times of a perceived abandonment his paranoia exacerbates, which results in a psychotic regression. James then states, "I am envious of my patients who are dying. I *want* to be them, why can't *I* get cancer and die?" James begins psychotically romanticizing the tragic position of his dying patients. *Not* the pain of his patients and *not* the fact that they are dying. But rather, James romanticizes and resents the *attention* his dying patients are being given by *him*. He is in fact envious of his own narcissistic psychotic projections. James also utilizes fusion, which is the opposite of abandonment, at least in its primary phase. For example, James frequently uses the names of family members and friends without offering an explanation as to who they represent in his life. This is one of many examples of a psychotic confluence that intersects like a Venn diagram between himself and the therapist. The therapist is assumed to know not only who the other is but also how the other is represented in James's inner world; "I am you and you are we and we are all together" (*I Am The Walrus*, The Beatles 1969). As James's psychotic process continues to devolve, his projective identifications become more rampant and regressed, frequently taking the form of James becoming jealous of his therapist's relationship with *him*.

—⚇—

A male patient who was sexually traumatized from an early age by a female cousin gains three hundred pounds to shield himself from anyone penetrating him. He of course creates a psychic locked-in syndrome with layer after layer of rage-saturated fat. After ten years he loses two hundred pounds fantasizing that he "will be happy," only to discover that he knows not who he sees in the mirror or his mind's eye. He stares at a reflection expecting to see a familiar face only to see the image of a stranger staring back equally as baffled by its counter reflection. He is awakening from a psychic coma. Asleep for many years, where over that time, the world changed. He speaks from the back of his throat, especially as he talks of his domineering, "incredibly successful mother" and his "barely adequate father."

No one noticed he was gaining more than fifty pounds a month beginning at age thirteen, becoming massively invisible.

—∞—

Many years ago, I saw a couple who had nothing. They lived in a trailer park, wore hand-me-down clothes, and ate when and if they could. During this particular session the wife described the husband becoming irate, which was not an unusual occurrence. He grabbed the telephone and threw it at her, barely missing her head and instead the phone sailed through the window where it landed with a plop in the front yard. That afternoon, as I was driving home, I came to a four-way stop. I lived just down the road from the original Wright Brothers estate. The homes on this particular corner were what might best be described as bucolic. Lampposts adorned with gargoyles and large well-manicured lawns announced affluence before the eye was drawn to the palatial magnificence of the mansions. As I sat waiting my turn to drive through the inter-section, I looked to my right at the façade of a well-tended Tudor when, crashing through the lavish, stained glass front window, sailed a telephone, landing with a plop on the Arcadian lawn.

—∞—

Someone told me how he used to trap lynx for their pelts. He de-scribed setting the trap and the particulars that were necessary to ensure luring the cat to the trap. It would take him a few days to make his rounds to all of his traps once they were set. If he was lucky, he said, each trap would have a trapped cat. Then he would come upon them and bash their heads in. This way he didn't damage the pelt. His anger was noted when he spoke of cats who would "twist all over hell," damaging their pelts, forcing him to "discard" them after having gone to all of the work to set the trap. He also said that he raised bobcats. "How do you tame a bobcat?" he asked. "Well I'll tell you. Bobcats and house cats have the same gestation period. So you get a bobcat and house cat pregnant at the same time. Then when the kittens are born, you drown the house cat kittens and put the bobcat kittens with the momma house cat. The momma house cat then tames the bobcat kittens." The defining of any organic being or object as "sub" entails its exploitation or demise in one form or another. It is necessary to first demonize whatever we are readying to exploit or destroy or to make *it* ("it" being a precursor to "them") not only unnecessary but us better off without it. There is much suffering that we ignore, deny, or collectively remain ignorant of. For example, one of the jobs in meat packing plants that is the most difficult to retain is that of the person who kills the cows. He has to lock the head of the cow in a *track restrainer* and then take a *captive bolt gun* which slams a steel bolt into the head of the cow, stunning it to death. Assuming that the cow's skull is perfectly aligned and the cow is *compliant* in the restraint. Usually the gunner is off a bit, as the cows are rarely accommodating, making the man manning the gun slam the bolt into their eyes, face, or side of the head. And of course, in descriptions of this type one thing that always get omitted are the sounds and smells. Being herded to one's death is not serene and there is no "dying with dignity" (whatever that fantasy happens to entail). Rather, it is the sounds and smells that usually undo the gunners. A bolt being powered by thousands of pounds of air pressure slamming into the face or eyes of a cow causes unthinkable pain and suffering. And, finally upon the moment of their death, they shit, emptying their bowels completely as they collapse onto a conveyor belt. Even the most hardened of men find themselves queasy and weak in the knees with the constant agonizing "moos" and cries of helplessness. They either embellish their denial and become even further entrenched in their callousness or begin to lose their minds in one way or the other, including becoming profoundly abusive to the cows, kicking or beating them, denying them a "quick and humane death" for causing a disruption in the workers' entrenched denial. Of course, all of this goes on beyond our senses. We go to the market and buy the benign *rump roast, New York strip steak*, or other *cuts* of meat. We don't typically go to the butcher and say, "I'd like a severed slab of meat from a tender portion of a well-fed dead cow." Euphemistic labels, which allow us to enjoy the spoils that result from the suffering not only of animals but also of other humans, serve as one of the foundations of collective denial. The greater the suffering associated

with the denial the more fluid the transition to psychopathic indifference. And, the greater the resulting pleasure that results from
the suffering, be it a good meal or making fortunes at the expense
of others and any other predatory act in between, the greater the
necessity of the indifference. *Tancred, the hero of Gerusalemme liberata,*
unknowingly kills his beloved Clorinda in a duel when she is disguised
as an enemy … But she has converted to Christianity before her death
… Perhaps we should convert all that can know of their promised
ascension as well as those who cannot before we kill them. Perhaps
the dinner prayer of "thanks" is denial in disguise.

—∞—

He was six, now he is twenty. He is gifted. His controlling, emas-
culating, passively-dominant mother expects him to "invent a cure
for cancer," but she lives a life of chronic disappointment. He always seemed short, even when it wasn't supposed to matter and sat
exaggeratedly bent over, seemingly always in some form of bodily
distress. He dressed with a well-defined negligence, taking great pains
to make himself look poor. His father smoked cheap pipe tobacco
and extolled his enterprising nature buying up broken tools for
pennies, returning them to the store for a replacement, and selling
them anew for dollars. The son, from six through twenty, watched
with pulled-back-shoulder pride at his father's ingenuity. As the lad
entered puberty his lack of regular bathing, active boyhood sweat
glands, and smell of cheap tobacco effectively repelled others from
any desire to be around him. He always maintained a stance of suffering born from an indifference of some kind of imagined trauma.
The mother and father insured their son's narcissistic impotent rage
by preventing him from ever having to face consequences appropriate for his age. "He shouldn't have to," they said. "He shouldn't
have to do *anything* he doesn't want to. He should be left alone to
do as he pleases. They'll see, when he invents a cure for cancer one
day, then he can say 'No, you can't have it,' to his naysayers, smashing
the cure on the floor." One afternoon, not long after he turned ten,
he looked unaffected and indifferent at my black, thrice-swollen
ankle, I having broken it the night before. I knew then that seeing

him as a smirkish antisocial was as intractable as what is now his fully blossomed psychopathic pedophilia. He remains one way or another his mother's and father's last opportunity to escape from obscurity and be the *someones* they believe they were destined to be.

—∞—

I knew a man who had a gambling problem. He was an industrialist billionaire who was a self-declared "big-time" high roller. He regularly admitted himself to only the finest treatment facilities declaring that he had a gambling addiction. The industrialist also prayed to his higher power to help him win when he played the ponies. But his favorite recreational activity was to hop what he called "gambling whore flights" that originated in Europe and ended up in Las Vegas. The flight had running card games, roulette wheels, and slot machines. It was also replete with some very high-class prostitutes. On this particular flight, the industrialist met a man who invited him to play a few hands of blackjack. Rather quickly my patient lost $8,000. When he went to settle up, his new friend waved him off and said, "Go have fun, we'll take care of it later." He went off and played with both the ladies and the dice. When the plane landed in Las Vegas the industrialist looked for the gentleman to settle up his debt. He was unable to find him and thought he would see him on the flight back. When he boarded the return flight the industrialist looked for the gentleman he was indebted to but he was nowhere to be found. Several days later he was in his office when his secretary buzzed him: "There are two gentlemen out here who say they have some business with you." The industrialist, always busy and hurried, huffily instructed his secretary to dismiss the men saying he did not have any appointments and more importantly did not feel like being bothered. The gentlemen insisted and finally the industrialist agreed to see them. They were dressed in expensive dark suits and carried shiny metallic brief cases. The industrialist asked them, "Who are you and what do you want? I don't know you." One of the well-dressed gentlemen politely said, "We are sorry to bother you and we certainly understand you are a very busy man, but we have been retained by the gentleman you played a private game of blackjack with on your recent trip to Las Vegas and we are here to collect." The industrialist did not hesitate and pulled out his checkbook and started to write a check for eight thousand dollars. He was again politely interrupted by one of the men who said, "Before you write the check we would like to show you something." He then pulled out a file that contained photographs of the industrialist's wife taking their children to school that morning, plus photographs of his children in the school cafeteria and several photos of his wife about town. The industrialist said he could feel his face go ashen when one of the men said, "You have a lovely family, I mean what a looker your wife is, and your children, ah what can you say about beautiful kids. Of course you know the amount was $8000 but now there is interest and finder's fees so $25,000 should cover it. These photographs and the negatives are yours to keep, I mean who wouldn't want pictures of such a lovely family. You will never hear from us again and of course we don't expect to hear from you." As the check was written one of the men pushed the photos and the negatives toward the industrialist's shaking hands. They placed the check in a brief case, saying it would be cashed through an offshore bank, and let themselves out. The industrialist immediately left his office and went home, telling his wife he wanted to take the family far away for a few days. She thought he was acting strange but he assured her he was simply appreciating his beautiful wife and their wonderful children.

—∞—

"Missa, Missa," Flo yelled. "Missa, Missa," she yelled again. "Everybody's a waitin' for you to come on down here." "Dinner's all ready too. Come on now and get on down here. Get your pretties on and get yourself a ready." The guests were becoming increasingly impatient. Sweet sixteen parties seemed to be happening every weekend now. There were more than one hundred guests at Missa Missa's. Everyone was there, even Senator Begley had come as a special favor to Missa Missa's step-daddy. "Go see what's taken that girl so long, Flo," Lovey Peal, Missa Missa's mother, said. "Oh Miss Lovey, you know that girl just comes when she want to, don't make no difference, seems not anyway." Then, interrupting the important talk of the attendees, a faint clap could be heard. Then another set of hands joined in, until more than two hundred hands were coming together, just as they were supposed to. The room was a roar. There standing on the landing above the ballroom was Missa Missa. Her beautiful blonde hair bouffanted on top of her head, and oh her gown. Lovey's head swayed unbeknown to her, to the soft strings of the quartet whispering Pachelbel's Canon in D Minor that encircled the elegant crowd of onlookers, longing for Missa Missa's descent into womanhood down the spiral staircase. Oh how the fresh, richly fragrant rose garland, entwined around the banister accented Missa Missa's finished poise. The silk taffeta of her dress was overlaid with a dainty, closely woven lace and delicate Akoya pearls. She stood at the rail, looking down at the crowd looking up at her. Missa Missa pressed her belly against the banister rail, leaning over just a bit and watched her crowd's happy hands, pleading bulging eyes and fat hungry lips. She cocked her head from side to side and an odd inquisitive countenance overtook her perfectly made-up face. The tinkle of a silver spoon striking a half-full champagne glass could be heard above the wanterors. "My dear friends," Lovey said, her voice now a quiver from more than sipping far too many *Krug Clos du Mesnil* so early in the afternoon, "I give you my beautiful daughter, on this, her special of special days, Missa Missa." And, on that, Flo began weaving through the well-wishers and congratulators. Senator Begley's wife was particularly annoyed at Flo's insolence when she failed to beg her pardon by pushing past her. Then, as Flo continued to display her ill manners, seemingly with each of the self-ascribed *sangre azul*, Missa Missa dropped the ball end of the tightly rolled up sheet that she was hiding behind her back. Impatience swelled among the crowd. Then curiosity overtook their impatience, as they looked up and saw Missa Missa tying one end of the finest, pure white 2000 thread count sheet to the rail of the banister, crinkling up one strand of the garland. Flo, trying to sidestep the photographer's tripod at the bottom of the stairs, looked up just as Missa Missa took hold of the other end of the sheet that she had, under the privacy of the canopy of her bed, fashioned into a noose. A collective gasp could be heard from the now troubled spectators. Then Missa Missa carefully slipped the noose over her high-piled hair, careful not to disturb a lock. Flo, especially for a big-butted Negro woman, rounded the top of the circular stairway with a deftness that Miss Lovey had never seen before. Usually Flo just spent her time complaining about this and that, never enough money here or never enough money there. Miss Lovey spent much of her time confounded by Flo's self-centered ways. But, Miss Lovey would later admit, Flo had earned her keep today. Over the rustle of the taffeta, Missa Missa could hear gasp after gasp from the inert looker-oners when she tossed her right leg over the top of the well-tended oak. She could even feel her stockings slipping a bit along the top rail. That Flo, she must have polished it up that morning before anyone had gotten up. Now Missa Missa was precariously balanced by one plump thigh resting on the balustrade. The tippy tips of her big toes of her little ankle-less feet pushed her one way then another, making her rock to and fro like a Weeble. Miss Lovey was beside herself having to witness the spectacle, just fretting something awful. Mr. William Potter, III, Miss Lovey's husband and Missa Missa's step-daddy, was apologizing profusely to Mr. Peterman. Mr. Potter had just been made a partner in Mr. Peterman's law firm. Peterman himself had taken a real interest in William. He was a rising star, going straight to the top rung in no time. After expressing his mortification to Mr. Peterman, William wormed his way through the poor distressed crowd to Miss Lovey and told her he was so angry that he could bite nails. Missa Missa should be locked up somewhere. He'd been telling that to Miss Lovey since right before she divorced Missa Missa's daddy, but she wouldn't have any of it. As he stood shaking his head, William remembered that just that morning, he'd told one of his pheasant hunting companions, he was so upset with Missa Missa that if she were one of his bird dogs and acted like she did he'd just shoot her and be done with it. William's bird hunting friend shook his head in understanding and said that he and his family had had to go through something awful like this a few years back. But it was with one of their live-in hired helps not one of their own offspring. "God forbid," he said. Just about the time that William's memory of the morning was dissolving and Miss Lovey's fretting was about to reach its crescendo, Flo's—bless her soul—well-worked arms seemed to come out of nowhere and tackle Missa Missa off of that smooth rail and plop her popped out butt right down onto the beautiful hardwood floor of the landing. Missa Missa was screamin' like a cat with tin cans tied to its tail and turpentine poured up its ass, Flo would later tell her husband Lemar. It didn't make no difference to Flo though. She'd handled ruffians before, she said to Lemar, and Missa Missa for sure wasn't *no* ruffian. Miss Lovey was beside herself again but this time with thankfulness that her guests didn't have to witness what could have been even more of a spectacle, if Flo hadn't grappled with Missa Missa. It was just no wonder that Miss Lovey was having to visit her doctor so much. The medicine he gave her to help her with her nerves just wasn't enough at times like this. But when she took it with one of William's juleps it made her nerves calm down and she was able to put her suffering aside, at least until it wore off. "I don't know how you do it," Miss Lovey's longest friend, Ninnie Bell, who'd been named after the great southern business woman, Ninnie Baird, would say over and over again. "I don't know either, Ninnie," Miss Lovey would say back and follow it up with, "It's just wearing me down to skin and bones," over and over, again and again. Ninnie'd nod right back, she was no stranger to suffering. The battles she'd been through with the first of four husbands when he fought for the Senate made her know what suffering truly was. Ninnie was able to understand Miss Lovey's angst like no one else, she would say. It was decided it'd be best to send Missa Missa to a boarding school of the highest repute, to help Miss Lovey cope with her suffering at having to endure her daughter, albeit of someone else's blood. William was insisting now and Flo, having spent most of her life with Miss Lovey and William and Miss Lovey and Missa Missa's daddy before, said that Missa Missa was just getting too big for her to handle, especially that she got winded now and had rheumatism so bad that she ached just about all the time and Lemar said he'd just about had enough of Flo coming home all bruised up. And so it was that Missa Missa went off to the best of the best boarding schools here and there, wreaking havoc and causing mayhem, savoring the angst like a bowl of hot grits laced with maple syrup. This remained Missa Missa's lifelong pattern of disrupting the lives of others and planting seeds of terror in everyone whose path she was invited to cross. A cogent feature of hysteria is the use of projective identification to create a fantasized existence of being part of a larger group, be it a dyad at its smallest to those much larger. This dissimulated identification allows one to create and play out—over and over again, a quasi-erotic performance, therefore giving the hysteric's distorted sexuality an ostentatious but crudely titillating disposition.

Vigils

"We all have to die of something," he says

"What?" I ask.

So we hear over and over, again and again. As we age… 'We all die of something.' What will that *something* be? Those who survive devastating illness say, "I got *my* cancer in…" "That was three years ago now." Like it was a cancer meant just for them.

"I got *my* heart attack on…" "I got *mine* ___ on…"

There is of course the desire for everything to *stop* all at once or to die in ones sleep. To drift off into a dream where we are called Forth by God, called forth to Heaven, St. Peter welcoming us to partake of the sweet eternal *repetitions* of ecstasy we knew in our lived lives.

"She's gone to a better place now," "Having pot roast with her Momma and Daddy…" The obituary read. Does the cow for the pot roast die over and over, again and again in this undying spectacle of everlasting gluttony? God's identity revealed for the first time as Adam Smith? Certainly, in this version of Heaven the cow doesn't seem to have much of a say about eternity.

The depths of emptiness can drive one to commit suicide of various forms, one direct where a life is ended abruptly or where the emptiness, either self or other imposed, becomes a form of psychological and emotional oxidation. The end result, the rotting away of the self and all of its attributes.

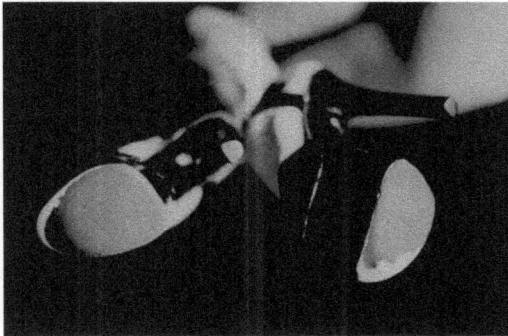

We All Want To Be Loved

He was about sixty or so, a short stocky man, who for all but a failed attempt at fucking was a virgin. When he was ten years old, he began having headaches. They came upon him suddenly, causing his immediate debilitation. His mother, becoming concerned, took him to a local physician who assured her that he was just looking for attention and, if he continued acting that way, should get "*slapped up the side of the head,*" giving him "*…something to have a headache about.*" He just wouldn't stop being a bad boy, getting slapped silly, but *nothing* abated his naughty behaviour, until on the third day, he suddenly lost consciousness. His mother, now realizing something was seriously wrong when she couldn't awake him, took him to a large medical center some four hours from their rural home. It was quickly discovered that he had a large mass on his cerebellum. He underwent six hours of neurosurgery. The final diagnosis was cancer of the cerebellum. Amazingly enough he was by definition cured. The surgeon had fully resected the tumor. The boy, however, was never quite the same. He became a loner, always withdrawn into himself, never wanting much to do with other people and upon turning eighteen decided to retreat to the Alaskan wilderness. He lived by himself in a cabin he'd roughed out by hewing downed trees. The lad made it a couple of years but decided to leave his cabin after being attacked by a large brown bear, resulting in substantial scalp wounds.

He settled on a small town where he would for the most part be left to live alone until one day it happened he fell in love. There he met the twins in a local second hand store. Never had he ever seen anything so beautiful in his life. Their thin black leather straps adorned with red rhinestones revealed that they had no shame...

He had always been unsuccessful in love until he met Lucy and Lacy. They, they accepted him for all of his foibles, *never* once leveling criticism. It was *them* and only *them* who would sit, watch him chain himself to the spigot in the bathtub, masturbate and flagellate himself without uttering so much as a sound.

His psychotherapist at the time, getting bored with listening to his day-in and day-out litany of woes, decided that his only way of becoming successful in love was for him to be rid of the burden of his virginity. The therapist believed that it was fortuitous that he had another patient who also had been unsuccessful at love—unless she was offered proper remuneration for her time limited affections, then she described her capabilities at loving as "*superb.*" The therapist convincingly said to his woeful patient, "Clearly *this* has been your problem," and arranged for his female patient to end what he saw as his male patient's lifetime of virginal strife. After having arranging for a hotel room and paying for his female patient's *superb* services, they met one night.

The loving, he was convinced, would have in fact been superb should he have been interested. But, try as she might, doing this and that, it was not meant to be. And given that it would mean so much to their mutual therapist, they agreed to say it *had been* a night of bliss and that they, now both having experienced something divine, found therapy no longer necessary. Upon reporting their momentous experience, the therapist was awash with deep satisfaction and bid them adieu. It was not long after the staged debacle that he met "Lucy and Lacy."

They would all take rides in his battered old truck to the deserted country side, him always packing his lunch while he saw them cast their sensual gaze, snuggling up close beside him as he drove, he being careful not to bump them when he downshifted. Spreading a blanket under a shade tree, he would take his sandwich out of the basket and lean back against the tree, ensconced in bliss. They always watched him eat.

He knew his bliss couldn't last forever. Lucy and Lacy would eventually break under the burden of the weight he put on them. One early morning, when he was preparing for a night away with just the three of them in a tent under the stars, he held them close to him, one on one side, one on the other, when, in a prelude to their night of ecstasy, he slipped Lucy on his left foot and Lacy on his right, and then standing up one time too many he put his full weight on their delicate heels collapsing them both to the ground. The crimson rhinestones began popping and rolling like marbles all over the floor, under the bed, the old wooden side table and tragically thorough a cracked floor board falling into the abyss of the crawlspace. He picked up Lucy and Lacy, held them close, comforting them in their demise. Later that day and shortly after he flagellated himself in his now lonely bathtub, he crawled around the floor, gathering up as many of the jewels as he could find, tenderly slipped Lucy and Lacy into a shoe box wrapped carefully in a pair of fresh linin bloomers and drove one last time, the twins sitting as close as they had ever sat beside him, their voices now silent. He buried them under the tree where they had taken many picnics, gently tamping down the earth to make sure an animal didn't disturb their remains.

In his desperation he began to look for another set of twins, he had been more than blessed to have had the time with Lucy and Lacy but now his loneliness was becoming overwhelming. No longer would just an unadorned pair of heels suffice, not after having known the elegance of Lucy and Lacy. He began taking day trips to the state capital, just a few hours away. He had looked around his little town, but the only shoes that expressed themselves in their uniqueness were snakeskin cowboy boots.

He began to walk the rotunda of the state house, always keeping his head down, wishing with his eyes for another Lucy, another Lacy. It seemed that the female legislators wore unassuming shoes. He said their well-fed ankles folded over the top straps, smothering what personality their shoes tried to express. But then he discovered the wives of the male law makers. "Ahhhhhh," he would say. When they came to meet their husbands for dinner, "oh the shoes they wore." *Always* high heels, *always* elegant and perhaps, just perhaps, sexier than Lucy and Lacy, although he felt guilty at even hinting at anything more than just a physical attraction.

He would follow a particular legislator and his wife, day in and day out for more than a month. Careful not to be seen, careful not to be found out. Until one early afternoon, when the police swooped down on him from all sides and arrested him for '*engaging in a course of conduct directed at a person or persons that serves no legitimate purpose and seriously alarms, annoys, or intimidates that/those person(s).*' During the interrogation he explained that he meant no harm, he only wanted to be close to the exquisiteness of the high heels, it was unfortunate that they were filled with feet other than his own, he said. Ultimately it was determined that he was no threat but he was forever banned from the statehouse unless he was there on official business, which was unlikely. He would spend the remainder of his life with his head down, not in despair but searching for another pair of twins who might be as perfectly fulfilling as Lucy and Lacy.

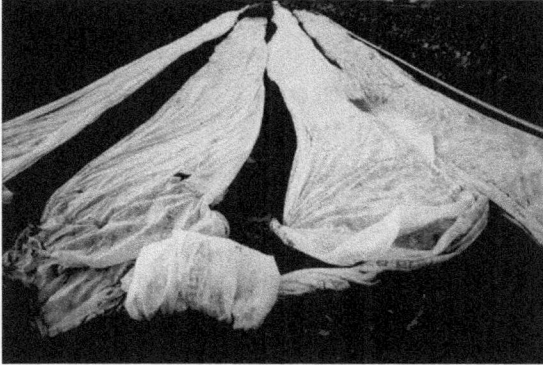

Gary

He was a very slight man, short, boyish and in those days 'homo-sexual.' He lived in a small Midwest town with deep conservative German roots. The folks of the town were proud of their heritage and in the cafes you could still hear the older men, who for this reason or that didn't go to the 'Great War,' talk of manning the towers constructed at the perimeters of the village, twenty-four hours a day looking out "for Jap planes," even though the town was a thousand miles inland.

He walked around the village dressed in a tuxedo. His always pale bare feet even in the coldest of weather contrasted dramatically against the blackness of his satin-striped tux pants. It was on a fall afternoon that he presented his thin, lumpy arm, saying that he had injected Tuinal (a combination of secobarbital sodium and amobarbital sodium) Subq, in dozens of sites. My office at the time had a massive window, fortunately at ground level, directly behind where the patient sat. In but a matter of minutes he began seizing in his chair, stood up in a tonic position and then threw himself through the plate glass window, crashing onto the sidewalk. Amazingly, he only had a few scratches on his face from flying glass, which was littered around him. Perhaps the tuxedo had protected him from the shards. He continued seizing until the ambulance took him to the local hospital.

The hospital ER was up a ramp and had a concrete abutment

where two pillars held the neon light indicating it was the hospital emergency entrance. The drop from the abutment was twenty feet.

He had stopped seizing after receiving lorazepam on the way to the ER. Upon being checked out a release order was signed after a few hours of stabilization. He called someone to come and get him and indicated that he would wait for them at the ER entrance. Outside of the ER he lifted himself up onto the wall of the abutment. Sitting there, with his legs pulled up against his chest, he suddenly began seizing again as more of the Tuinal broke free. His body stiffened and he threw himself off the abutment falling onto the tarmac below, fracturing both hips and breaking both ankles. He would never walk without a pronounced limp and would now clinically *need* a lifetime of narcotic pain medication.

There is no moral to the story per se, but it does go to show that there are many folks who simply in this life will never 'get a break' (so to speak) and that the countless flowery clinical histories that we so often see pandered are a way of narcissistically making psychotherapists/analysts more relevant than perhaps we should at times consider ourselves. Yet, we must believe in what we do if we are to bring some semblance of relief to those who seek us out to ameliorate some of their suffering as well as some of our own.

Ranting

Of late there is a movement implying that the *'treatment of choice'* for schizophrenia is psychoanalysis. My thoughts on this are combined with how we as clinicians address boredom and hopelessness with patients who by definition 'will never get better.' Or those who present as helpless but we deny our helplessness in the face of their helplessness and rather project fantasies of 'improvement' to maintain our self-worth.

Up until the advent of neuroleptics not much 'worked' with schizophrenics or psychotics. We tried dunking them, inducing insulin shock, CO2, for lack of a better word—*poisoning*, praying over them, putting them on an island by themselves and declaring their psychotic process to be so *deeply* insightful that only fellow schizophrenics could understand each other, declaring that they were *double-bound* and that the only way to untwist them through *reparenting* (baby bottles were in vogue during the reparenting), and the list goes on.

Then phenothiazine, i.e. Thorazine, and its derivatives came along in the early 1950s. Mellaril, a buffered concoction of Thorazine, was the next big jump. The neuroleptics didn't make a leap again until 1958 but didn't see wide spread use until the mid-1960s. And so the development of neuroleptics has continued with there now being more than twenty. The problem of course with each and every one is the profound side-effect profile: Dry mouth, being the most benign, while tardive-dyskinesia and potentially *neuroleptic malignant syndrome* being the most devastating—i.e. potentially death. Being chronically crazy is hard. If a therapist has had much experience with folks who are in fact crazy, they do not come into our offices and say, "*My God I LOVE being insane, I love the voices in my head and I love sitting here and seeing you look like a skeleton in a casket being consumed by maggots.*" Actually, they don't. Rather they talk about the terror of being out of their minds. Of what we know as reality being so fucked up that their ability to order lunch without being paranoid that the cook is poisoning their food. I remember one fellow who stayed in his house, day in and day out, wrapped in tin foil to ward off the radio beams being broadcast at him by not only the government but the aliens who *actually* run the government. The advent of the medications offered some semblance of relief, albeit with wretched side effects, but for most that was at least some sense of reprieve from the wretchedness that fucked with minds.

There have been many books written by those who live within this world of madness, who discuss the terror, the paranoid, the inability to maintain relationships and the profound isolation and loneliness they constantly struggle with. I have yet to see a book on *Living with the Enlightenment of Schizophrenia.*

Now there is a 'new' perspective that psychoanalysis 'should' be the treatment of choice for psychotic process. Melanie Klein is often quoted in regard to this. However, there are questions about Melanie Klein's own psychotic process. I believe that we have to be extremely cautious that we don't project our own madness on the patient regardless of their diagnosis and declare it an interpretation. The alleviation of symptoms is not necessarily the focus of a psychotherapy. Rather, it seems as though exploration and enhancing the self, *whoever* it may be, is far more efficacious in terms of achieving some relief of the 'stated problem' as to why someone came into treatment in the first place. However, a reality is that no one who *is* schizophrenic has ever become *not* schizophrenic either by medication, psychotherapy or psychoanalysis, any more than someone who is borderline has become not borderline.

We ultimately are who we are and what we are. To be schizophrenic means that the person will be struggling with hallucinated, delusional and paranoid process throughout their entire lives. They will distort what is typically understood to be reality and will *not* view their struggles as 'enlightenment.' A recent work by a prominent author discuss how he now sees psychoanalysis as the treatment of choice for schizophrenics and discusses spending hours and sometimes days on end being with patients who are having a breakdown. Ultimately I admire his kindness but am also suspicious of his voyeurism and countertransference to his confrontation with helplessness. Schizophrenia is described by patients as "Hell." A nightmare of existence. Just because we have a clinical theory as to what *may* work we must be careful not to again project our fantasies on the patient and inhibit their ability to use a treatment regimen that may actually provide some form of relief.

Repeatedly psychotherapy seeks out either new 'trends' or re-treats to historical theoretical constructs and 'discovers' new ways of making them applicable. Carl Whitaker, John Warkentin and Virginia Satir in the late 1950s engaged in bottle feeding patients suffering with schizophrenia as an attempt to rebirth and ultimately reparent them, giving them a more nurtured experience, resulting in whatever the word 'cure' means. This was a disastrous failure, as was R. D. Laing taking a similar approach with schizophrenic patients treating themselves.

The countertransference of boredom and the anxiety associated with remaining relevant within the treatment paradigm has received little attention. Yet, we continue to see this dynamic emerge repeatedly in supervision as well as in education programs, at all levels. Physicians who are credentialed in specialties other than psychiatry have to confront this day in and day out. Oncologists treat terminal patients hourly, neurosurgeons lose eight-five percent of their patients. Dermatologists up until the late 1980s felt some sense of prophylaxis and then came AIDS, lymphomas and *Kaposi's sarcoma*. And these specialties from day one of their residencies discuss and prepare as much as possible the physician with the inevitable fact that many of their patients will die. I have *yet* to find one psychology/psychotherapy program that even remotely raises the issue of the inevitability of encountering folks who live with profoundly debilitating, and most often than not, barely treatable mental illnesses. By untreatable, I do not mean that symptoms cannot be at time mitigated, however *we* will *not* as clinicians ever *cure* any patient we see of a serious mental disease. This does not imply that we are unimportant in our patients' lives nor does it imply that our work is not valuable. It does imply that we must as therapists be able on a personal level to internally manage our inevitable confrontations with impotence. This can ultimately only be done with supervision from someone who in fact has dealt with their (our) own issues of irrelevancy, impotence and a desire to 'help.' Which ultimately is a desire to secure power/relevancy through an interpersonal clinical dynamic by seeing the patient not for who they are but for how we *want* them to be or fantasize how 'they could be.' I have heard supervisees state countless times over the years, "They aren't doing what I say in therapy, they won't take their medication, they won't go to group, they won't…""I guess they *don't want to change.*"

I often see clinicians of all disciplines move towards a more 'spiritual' path with their patients. Others seek to become a friend in the patient's time of need. However, this pseudo altruistic friendship tends to deteriorate when the patient stops paying them. I remember discussing a case with a family physician many years ago who had a very low functioning borderline patient in their practice. The patient continued to place demands on the physician for a more effective 'cure' to relieve their symptoms of loneliness and despair. "*Clearly,*" they said, the only answer for the physician was to take the patient into their household and give them a "real life" example of how "healthy" people live, therefore "…allowing this to bleed over into the psyche of the patient." The outcome was as nightmarish as one might imagine.

I want to emphasize that I am not attempting to hawk what has historically been referred to as the 'medical model.' There is a mountainous amount of clinical and statistical evidence demonstrating equally the questionable ineffectiveness of medications. Part of where the problem lies is again in coming face-to-face with the helplessness and boredom that clinicians encounter when confronting situations whereby they have little or no ability to intervene in a way that will reflect back a personal satisfaction or a narcissistic rendering. When the pendulum swings to proselytizing on either side, a blindness develops and from that lack of vision the patient then becomes a pawn in a sophisticated counter-transference battle for the patient's soul.

Mark

Many years ago now I received a call from a social service agency asking me if I would consider accepting as a patient an eight-year-old boy who was diagnosed with "primitive personality disorder and encopresis." I stated that I would consider it if we could staff the case with all of the principals involved, including the child.

As I sat in the conference awaiting the young boy to arrive with his foster parents, I listened to the social service representative asserting that he had been "smearing feces for years." His 'chart' sat in front of me, it was at least ten inches thick. He had been removed from his biological mother when he was two years old and upon a quick look into the medical record he was diagnosed by a state social worker at *two years old* with "…Having a primitive personality and pooping his pants." "He is also stubborn and *won't* get potty trained." I expected when he arrived a child who was going to come in and begin chewing the woodwork off the wall. Instead a young man walked in the door, promptly came up to me and said, "I don't know who you are, I'm Mark." His social service worker told him to "Sit down and just be quiet while the adults talk." At this point I was far less interested in the *adults* than in Mark.

Figuring that he knew that everyone else knew his history I told him that these folks had asked me to in essence take a look at him. I also said that I was not interested in taking a 'look at him' but was interested in seeing if he and I might like to spend some time talking and if not then that was okay too. I was also interested in why at eight he was till pooping his pants. He couldn't help it, he said. He had been in the new foster parents' custody now for a year or so. They were reasonable people and interested in Mark. The foster mother said she didn't agree with "everyone" saying he had been "deliberately" soiling himself. The social service person told me to read the boys chart and "…that will tell you all you'll need to know." I respectfully rejected her mandate. Mark was forth-coming and said that he had bowel movements every four to five days and that his underwear was always soiled because he "leaked poop" all the time. He had no friends because he smelled "really bad" all the time. I asked the social service worker if she had ever had Mark checked by a physician. She promptly produced a note from a pediatrician who said he had checked the boy when he was six and that there was nothing wrong with him. He was "Just being difficult for the attention." I suggested that Mark get examined by a pediatric gastroenterologist. The social service person disagreed and said it was a waste of time and money. There is a medical condition called *Hirschsprung's disease* that causes a megacolon to develop do to a lack of epithelial cells, which produce elasticity in the bowel track. These cells, like the epithelial cells found in our cheeks, is what allows for peristalsis to occur, not different from when one 'pops their cheeks.' In Hirschsprung's disease the cells do not exist or there is a depletion of them, which results in pockets to develop in the bowel track capturing fecal material as it moves through the bowel track, resulting in impaction. Bowel fluid 'leaches' around the impaction which results in leakage. It also results in massive bowel movements every four to five days.

After much debate the social service worker 'permitted' the young man to go for an examination to a physician I recommended. Upon examination the young man was transported via helicopter to a larger hospital where he underwent surgery to excise segments of his colon where there was significant breakdown of the bowel wall and he was at risk for peritonitis.

Clearly, there is *no* diagnosis of primitive personality disorder and unless a child is significantly developmentally disabled the diagnosis of encopresis at two is simply malpractice. Mark is now in his late twenties and has been 'problem free' for many years.

Vaporous Longings

"Come to me," she gestures. Her hands waving him towards her, offering herself, as he imagines her to be. And then, upon his approach, her arms open, offering up *Adam's Ale* as an alchemist's elixir. He steps into the *welcoming* and reaches for the maternal promise. *Swoosh… Swoosh… Swoosh…* His arms enfold unto themselves, grasping hands squeeze the vapors as the smoke passes through his fingers, *swoosh… swoosh… swoosh…* "Why won't you come to me!!!" he hears. "I am trying, Mother!" he screams. His arms flail like an *Algren boxer*.

She can be *seen* in his ocular desperation, be it the mother of his birth or the successor mothers as his life has chronologically moved along. And, in those moments when the fingertips of progeny encircle the maternal fingertips with the longing expectation of affective asylum, the son is thrust into a psychic nimbus, only to discover that the mother of one's fantasy has quickly devolved into *Baby Jane Hudson*. There is nothing to grasp onto, nothing on which to hold, except phantasy broadcast through projective-identification. And yet even the phantasy is unclear in whatever idyllic representations it may hold, instead tainted with opaque *maternal covenants*.

Projective-identification came to life in the form of a well-rehearsed Athenian tragedy. The rostrum of her hysterical performances rotates her through the audience of her life, taking on the imago of this character and that, penetrating herself into the fabric of each attendee at each production; one histrionic event being enveloped by the other, until she is lives adrift on a Mobius strip.

It has become vogue to downplay or even dismiss with prejudice the impact of an unresolved oedipal dynamic. However, the ensuing rage and issues with control and domination that play out over a lifetime cannot be understated with their lineage being traced directly to the lack of oedipal resolution and from this failure of resolve ensues at times maniacal projective-identifying states. For a matter of clarification, one can importantly consider *projectively-identifying* as one who seeks to identify projections in the other for purposes of exploitation.

Jane

An individual I once knew, perhaps we could call her Jane, came from a wealthy, blue blood family. In the continuity of her complex history lay a wake of destroyed lives, based upon well-constructed false accusations and paranoia. Her step-father was almost destroyed by her denunciations of ongoing sexual assaults. None of which were true, which was later acknowledged while relating when she accused a dentist of similar behavior. Once, she briefly 'fell in love' with a man, who upon one of their first impassioned sexual encounters was shocked when she began screaming that he was raping her, and then ran outside naked and called the police. He was booked, later released with the charges being dropped. However, now and forever he will have a police file with the accusation of a sexual assault, "…charges dropped". The woman was adopted when she was around one year, her birth mother being a young sixteen-year-old girl whose giving birth to a bastard would forever stain her. The little girl was adopted by a wealthy east coast couple. The couple offered means that the little girl could have never hoped for: the finest of the finest finishing schools on her path to becoming a proper lady. As time went on the child became increasingly enamored with her daddy. Mother became increasing more resentful of the little girl constantly vying for daddy's affections. The little girl then foresaw the advantages of splitting the mother and father in order to successfully win her father's attentions. The mother and father's relationship had begun to dissolve amongst his many affairs and political ascension. The mother now began to become increasingly more resentful of her daughter and her husband's displaced affections. Her father was sure of his daughter's devotion while the mother was equally assured of her "evilness." The family maid was also aligned with the mother. Hence, and many years later, the maid's daughter was almost destroyed by a well-developed pattern of lies that resulted in the daughter's child being taken by authorities, while the daughter was investigated for the distribution of drugs—a fabrication that was well tented in its timing, construction and execution.

Later, when she went to college, Jane expanded her unresolved oedipal rage and then began to concoct stories of abuse against her step-mother, whom she convinced her father was likely poisoning him in order to acquire his fortune. It would be necessary for her return home and help him to manage his life. First, however, she must rid herself of her dog, which she left outside to freeze to death after throwing water on it. She found her pet stiff the next morning. It wasn't long after that she relocated to her hometown and began terrorizing not only her step-mother, but all of the members of her family. Once, when she was able to "hunt down" her biological mother, the family felt some relief with her rage being now temporarily disbursed.

The birth mother had been sixteen when she engaged in an indiscretion that resulted in her giving birth to an illegitimate daughter. Upon birth, the *bastard* child was immediately placed up for adoption and was never spoken of again until the unwelcomed knock at the door many years later. "There she was, my mother, standing there, looking so much like me," she would say. The mother had clearly struggled financially, which was demonstrated by her living conditions and her "uncultured" manner of dress. "I waste more money in a month than she makes in a year." And, upon accepting her mother's amends she suggested they go out to dinner someplace "nice." There she ordered and ordered and ordered until her belly felt it was ready to burst and then she demanded her mother pay the bill to demonstrate her good will and sorrow for having abandoned her. Her mother sat counting pennies from her change purse. She had just the right amount. Then Jane promptly stood up and left the restaurant, leaving her mother, abandoned, embarrassed at not having money for a tip.

Once they arrived back at the house, Jane's mother said she thought it best if they not see each other again, having opened old wounds that she wished to remain closed. Jane said no, she thought it best not only if she continued to visit but also to meet the rest of the family. The mother was mortified and begged Jane not to remain or to return. Jane stood steadfast.

Over the next three years Jane visited once a month, showing up for Thanksgiving and Christmas, becoming enraged when each member of her family failed to give her a present that was "nice enough" to earn "my thank-you." The mother discovered that she had stage-four cancer and kept it from Jane, and upon Jane's arrival for Thanksgiving the fourth year of their "reunion", she discovered that the mother had died, not so much leaving a note. Jane returned to her other home, "the expensive one" and exponentially rekindled her reign psychic terror.

The Strange Case of Mr. Smith's Pedophillic Obsessive-Compulsive Disorder

History:

Mark Smith came to me stating that he was suicidal because he could no longer manage the ascension of feelings regarding being sexually abused when he was a young boy. Upon arrival, Mark sat down on my couch and began immediately decompensating, gasping for breath, as he told of having been "sexually abused" at the age of six by his eight-year-old female cousin.

The "abuse" lasted until Mark was just a few months shy of turning thirteen, when his cousin came to him and said "they" could no longer have sex as she had been found out and was being sent away to a psychiatric facility. Mark was devastated, having gone from feeling abused to "falling in love" with his cousin right about the age of eleven.

He only saw her one other time. When he turned twenty-one Mark and his cousin's path crossed at a family reunion, she was now married and pregnant with her first child. Mark was devastated.

About two months after Mark was "jilted" by his cousin, he began eating copious quantities of food. He would wake up in the middle of the night, sneak out of the house and walk to an all-night diner, where he would eat several full meals. In two years he went from one hundred forty-five pounds to more than three hundred seventy-five pounds. His parents were dismayed, unsure of what to do. However, he was never evaluated by a psychotherapist. He was also now ostracized by his friends and rarely left his room, except to eat and then retreat. Mark also compulsively masturbated, describing, "I'd jerk off more than a dozen times a day, other than eating that was all I was doing, thinking about my cousin.

"Seeing her naked, then as I got older, I couldn't remember what she looked like, so I started looking at pictures of adolescent girls, but the older I got, I started realizing that I was becoming a man and I was still jerking off to adolescent girls, then I started obsessing that I was a pedophile, so then if I was able to resist and not jerk off then I knew I wasn't a *pedo*, but if I did then I knew I must be even though I knew I wasn't, I was only interested in my cousin and even looked for pictures of girls who looked like her and that took a lot of time and I had to go through thousands of pictures to try and find ones that were similar.

"Then I couldn't stop, I had to constantly see if I was turned on to the pictures and movies and like I said if I was then I knew I was a pedophile and if I didn't then I knew I wasn't.

"But, I never ever, not even one time, ever touched a child or an adolescent, with the exception of my cousin."

This obsessive vortex spun Mark out of control well into his late twenties, when two detectives served him with a warrant to search his home and confiscate his computers. When he came to see me for his first appointment, it was five days after his encounter with the police. However, he never mentioned this had occurred until four months later, when on a Thursday afternoon, I received a panicked phone call from his father telling me Mark had been arrested for *"the sexual abuse of children"* and *"possession of child pornography."* A successful prosecution of these charges would result in Mark being imprisoned from "twenty years to life."

Clinical Perspective:

OCD, by definition is *not* a simplistic clinical phenomenon that is simply definable by its manifest symptom constellation. One of the hallmarks of OCD is a *circularity of thoughts* and further compounding on this conceptualization is the notion that these thoughts are by definition *chemical thoughts* that are driven in part not just by neurology but also by intrapsychic process.

OCD is often an attempt to ward off some form of magically considered negative or disastrous outcome if the behavioral ritual associated with the circularity of thoughts is not completed. There is usually a secondary ascension of anxiety that emerges when the *required* response to the thought/behavior is challenged, either externally or internally. There lies within an individual a dynamic interplay of confusion as to a construct of imagined possibility *verses* actual probability. The P-OCD becomes a disorder set within an equally conceptualized conflict of '*Am I, Am I not?*' There is a delusional distortion that is consequentially visible, but only interruptible in retrospect not prospect if you will. The inferences that are thusly inherent in the aforestated dynamic are established, likely as, at least in part, a cerebellar cartography resulting in a confused and distorted *pattern* of reasoning.

In the case of P-OCD, what emerges often takes the form of:

A history of a sexually charged *ongoing* childhood experiences with the comingling psychological dynamic of guilt/embarrassment/illicit stimulation and/or trauma bonding. This constellation of exposure frequently involves sexualized contact with a peer of equal to slightly older chronological age. When examining these relatively few case histories, there is also evidence of a relatively sudden dissolution of the traumatic bond with the associated object.

As well there is also a history that is commonplace of the emergence of a *βhemolytic streptococcus* infection (which is highly correlated to the sudden onset of OCD as well as the development of PANDAS). Once the traumatic bond is severed, the sexual fantasies associated with the originating dynamic becomes the only means of *replication* of the object itself.

As part of the history there is also, primarily because of the ongoing nature of the sexualized relationship, a stagnation of psychosexual development. Therefore the ability to successfully transition through what is typically considered normal psychosexual development is thwarted, resulting in a psychosexual fixation that is consistent to within a few years of the age of the severing of the traumatic bond. At the age of twelve or thirteen, for example, would not be considered aberrant, should a boy begin to engage in the viewing of hebephiliac or ephebophilic pornography. However, now combined with a virulent OCD, the behavior increases exponentially while increasingly entrenching what may best be termed a 'craving' for an object with age and physical attributes similar to the object of the original traumatic bonding.

Where this becomes unusual lies in the fact that the individual with P-OCD is not by *character* a psychopath.

Within the P-OCD dynamic there also exists a cauldron of anxiety that dramatically tumefies and ascends as the chronological age of the young man moves toward adulthood causing profound internal conflict at the lack of resolution of the psychosexual disruption. The circularity of the OCD aspects of the dynamic is often misidentified as 'depression' or not infrequently 'bipolar disorder.' Thus further confounding the ability to effectively treat what more precisely is the etiology of the disturbance. With this foundation let us begin to explore the intrapsychic dynamics associated with the P-OCD dynamics.

The intrafamilial dynamics are observed typically to be a parental dyad that appears to be actively involved in their child's life. However, on closer examination it is not uncommon to see a more passive father and a more dominate mother, who when they observe their son behaving oddly completely miss the behavioral and emotional cues that would result in providing help that would speak to the child's needs based upon an accurate interpretation of his symptoms. Rather, what we see are misguided attempts to help the child that often take the form of, "if only you would…", or "have you tried to…" when dealing with the overt presentation of their symptomatology.

In P-OCD the individual is unable to advance beyond their developmental stagnation. They *are* attracted to sexualized objects who reflect the developmental position where they are stagnated. At the age of where the P-OCD begins to manifest the individual is not by definition engaging in pedophillic behaviour as his sexual interest is in fact age and developmentally consistent. However, as s/he begins to advance in chronological years their interest in younger children does not mature with age. They are chronically plagued by anxiety that cannot 'be shaken' at the interest in adolescents or preadolescents. Rather, the anxiety now begins to become overwhelming. The individual plagued with P-OCD unconsciously develops a *pattern* to view CP and if he is *unable* to become erect and masturbate, in the case of a male then he is "not a pedophile," but if he does become erect and masturbates then he "*is* a pedophile." In the case of the female, the *pattern* of the behavior is defined by vaginal wetness and orgasm. This cyclical dynamic thus becomes a tormentor in and of itself. It becomes a dynamic that one has profound difficulty in severing. Rarely if ever does someone who operates within the confines of this dynamic become a 'hands-on' offender. Typically what emerges is severe depression usually accompanied by active suicidal thoughts at the thought of '*ever touching a child.*'

In these individuals it is rare to find someone who does not express severe physical symptoms (nausea, etc.) at even the suggestion that they are a pedophile. When they have been discovered possessing CP by law enforcement and are adjudicated to sexual offender groups (either on probation or upon being incarcerated) they define those "...*other group members as sickos and disgusting*"—most particularly those who have engaged in *hands-on* sexual assaults of children/adolescents.

Compulsive masturbation is also inherent as part of the P-OCD process. The greater the ascension of the anxiety associated with the P-OCD thoughts and the viewing of CP the more the individual *must* engage in compulsory patternistic masturbation. It is not uncommon for someone struggling with P-OCD to become so confused as to what in fact "...turns me on" that they begin to have difficulty with getting and maintaining erections, regardless of their age.

Illegality:

Clearly the viewing and or possession of CP in most developed countries is in fact illegal and punishable by severe penalties resulting in what can be substantial prison terms.

P-OCD is not an exception to the findings of most courts. The law is as the law is. In only one case that I am aware has the federal court taken an 'interest' in the adjudication of an individual convicted of P-OCD related possession of CP. In the case I am referencing the only strategy that was assumed would have any efficacy would be to in essence to 'try' the case outside of the courtroom. To take any CP case in front of a jury is a *guaranteed* conviction and a guaranteed handing out of a very harsh sentence. Therefore, in the case referenced the prosecution was brought into the case for discussions within twenty-four hours of the arrest of the individual. The first factor that must be addressed was, from a clinical perspective, a negative countertransference of the law enforcement personnel to the evidence, namely the CP. There was no attempt in this case to deny that the individual was in the possession of CP or that he had in fact obtained it. However, there was immediately an attempt to educate the prosecutor about P-OCD. This was a steep grade to traverse as first and foremost to understand is not the job of a prosecutor. Rather, their job is to secure a conviction. The conviction however would in essence go unchallenged, however, the educational process with regard to the court would take two years in order to bring about the best possible results for the patient/client in this particular case. There were weekly reports submitted to the defense attorney, who then forwarded them to the prosecutor's office as a way of maintaining involvement in the case and not allowing the case to be 'just another case on the docket.' The most difficult aspect of managing the case was again the *content* of the CP. There were forty-three thousand still images of children of all ages being victimized and seventy-two highly graphic videos. This was a massive number. The detectives in the case were pushing for what would have amounted to life in prison (fifty plus years without parole). However, the key was to maintain strictly a *continual flow* of information back and forth, always with an educative compo-nent, combined with an empathic stance toward the prosecutors attempting to understand what we were developing as the clinical dynamics associated with the case.

After an eighteen month period the prosecution agreed to placement in the most minimum federal prison in the United States for a period of twenty-four months and concurrent placement in the drug and alcohol treatment program affiliated with the prison. Before the individual went to serve his sentence a substance abuse evaluation was completed in order to facilitate placement in the prison substance abuse program as soon as possible, as it usually takes a minimum of three months to have an internal evaluation completed and to find a bed. Completing the evaluation prior to entering the prison reduced the individual's time to enter the program to three days. Ultimately the individual was released to a step down facility after eighteen months and was then released fully back to the community, to serve out an eight-year supervised probation. It is not uncommon that clinical aspects of a criminal case are structured in an *ad hominem* fashion by both the defense and the prosecution. However if a dynamic can be established between the opposing parties that facilitates what can amount to as an *undefined agreement of cooperation*, then the outcome for the individual who is now enmeshed in the legal system and facing potentially many years of incarceration can be mitigated.

Murder by Shadow

In 1934 the autochthonous master of the macabre Abraham Merritt wrote *"Creep, Shadow, Creep"* about a Demoiselle, *Dahut the White*, who possessed the ability to give life to and thus control the lives of *shadows*. The shadows became her minions to do her bidding and when she tired of them cast them back to simply being physic dependent silhouettes.

Billy was about thirty or so, tall, blond, 'modelish' in appearance, delicate in his features, deeply invested in presenting himself as an always benign victim. He elicited great sympathy for the tragedies he had had to endure in his short life. First and foremost were the suicides of three of his roommates. One right after the other. There was the first, Carl, who when Billy had just turned twenty-one had overdosed in Billy's bathtub. Billy walked in and found him after coming home and noticing water pouring from under the bathroom door. He was quite dead, so there was no reason to attempt reviving him. "It was sooo tragic," he said, glancing up from looking down through a demure tearfulness. It was several years before he was able to overcome the trauma and take in another boarder. His second boarder, "Very fragile," he would say, and "Deeply sensitive to anything critical, even when you were trying to be helpful.

"Benny," was his name, who after only three months of living with Billy threw himself out their apartment window and landed atop a bus with a decidable plop. "Dead as a door nail," Billy said he was. Again, he looked up from his crouch, the dozen or so eyes of the group now affixed with *his* grief, and again he said, it was another several years before he could bring himself to take another "roomie." The third and "I've finally had it with roommates," he added, was much older than him and, "he almost killed me with his *incessant* whining…" Until on another fateful day, Billy arrived home to find "Alan hanging in *MY* closet.

"Can you believe it? He hung himself with one of my *good* ties. And the cops, bastards they are, wouldn't even return it. 'Oh we *think* it's suicide but we just can't be sure so we can't return a piece of what may be evidence,'" the cops told Billy.

Shortly afterwards, Billy became acutely depressed and suicidal himself and ended up in the hospital where within a short period of time he gained the *sympathies* of the hospital staff, aghast at how one person could have such a string of misfortune.

After a brief period of time, and while he was sitting in a group therapy session with a blanket pulled around him like a shroud, the therapist looked at him. "May I tell you what I see when I look at you?" the therapist asked.

"Yes," Billy said, "I would like to know."

"I see you lying in front of a tombstone… Asleep, and… *gloating.*"

Billy became enraged, throwing the blanket from around his shoulders, standing and screaming at the therapist. "You motherfuck-er!" he screamed. "Why don't *YOU* move in with me motherfucker and see what happens? You think you're more powerful than *I* am, do YOU!?" The therapist sat; the group moved from being controlled through sympathy to stark terror. "I think you're a con man," the therapist said. "I also, just from the miniscule amount of time I have met you, think are likely *far* less suicidal than you are homicidal. I know, I know, don't rush to judgment and all that, but… I don't trust you and what you are saying and the effect you are having on this group is as though you drugged them.

"You all look barely conscious except when Billy is talking, then you perk up and then when he stops talking you lose consciousness again. So something is not kosher here."

"*You're* a motherfucker," Billy said again. But, in all of his raging, Billy, not one time, said, "You are wrong." Mostly he just said moth-erfucker repeatedly. He stormed out of the group and told how he had been abused by the therapist. Listening, the psychiatrist was incensed that he had been treated so badly and likely that he had suffered secondary trauma from the confrontation. Over the next few hours great discussion occurred between staff members, who for some reason were beginning to question Billy's impact on the psychiatric hospital staff. And, in an odd shift of fate, and just as the sun began to go dark for the night, two deputies arrived with an arrest warrant for Billy for first degree murder of Alan. It seemed as though Alan had ingested enough benzodiazepines that he was in essence dead and most certainly could not have hung himself, at least without assistance. It also seemed that while Billy was in the hospital, the police had executed a search warrant and found a thermos with only Billy's finger prints containing a concoction with a "…horse dose of benzodiazepines," the deputy said when he was discussing the case with the staff. Later on, Billy was charged with being an accomplice to the deaths of Carl and Benny. The prosecutors knew the charges wouldn't hold, as murder by projective-identification is impossible to prove, but, it proved helpful in "weaseling a confession from Billy" for Alan's murder, who as Billy said, "…Was a *real* pain in the ass, I hated the motherfucker from the first time he showed up at my door, answering the ad I'd put in the paper. I mean, I even said in the ad that I was a warm and sympathetic landlord, but *HE* was ridiculous!" Billy is still in prison. It is unknown if any of his cell mates have committed suicide.

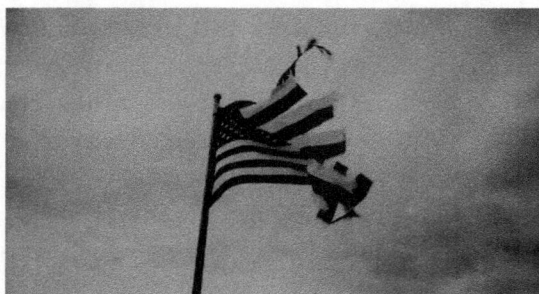

Oh Donny Boy

With the multitude of discussions occurring about Donald Trump's 'narcissism,' a broader clinical perspective regarding *devolving* sociopathic narcissism may be in order. What has been errant in the discussion is that Trump is by definition not *just* 'narcissistic.' Trump's narcissistic manifestations also appear to be well entrenched in sociopathy and an intractable psychotic/neurologic process.

From a pragmatic standpoint an 'amount' of narcissism is necessary for being successful as it is for living. What is imperative to understand, is that our now president appears to have a definable mental illness that appears to manifest as a narcissistic personality disorder *with* sociopathy.

This primitive form of narcissism is by definition an intractable and realistically *untreatable* mental illness that even under the most ideal of clinical circumstances is *only* manageable at best. In Mr. Trump's case it is manifest in apparently shady business dealings and in politically oppressive ways. However, the etiology is not business per se or political by nature but rather psychological. What we see manifest in individuals who are primitively bound within this commingled pathological structure takes on the following dynamics:

Sociopathic narcissism is not a diagnosis that is mysterious or one that looks like magical realism. Rather, like most clinical processes, it has a relatively well defined pathological structure (while having almost a complete lack of intrapsychic structure) and is also relatively predictable, *once* the individual has revealed enough of how their sociopathic narcissistic dynamics manifest. First, as we have seen demonstrated repeatedly, and using Mr. Trump as an example, narcissists seek out others who will behave in an obsequious manner, not just while in their physical presence but also who will *parrot* their projections while out of their physical presence.

A primary source of anxiety that lives within the sociopathic narcissist is a terror of *ruinous disillusionment* which would ultimately terminate in a catastrophic exposure of what is in essence a *fraudulent* existence. As the risk of exposure intensifies, be it in a dyad or more macro group structures, their intrapsychic constellation becomes increasing more fragile and their manifest behavior becomes more erratic.

It is here that we can now begin to explore how *projective-identification* is an integral aspect to the sociopathic narcissist. Projective-identification can be understood as *the process of consciously or unconsciously interlacing affectively charged psychic residue (introjects of a malignant nature) and their accompanying behaviors with counter-resonating, introjectively identified psychic material that already exists within a host and is primed to be collectively echoed. In other words, projective-identification is the implanting of emotionally charged psychological residue into another introjectively fertile person or collective body, and importantly so, whose own counter-resonating introjective residue already exists within.*

The sociopathic narcissist does not deliberately put themselves in front of those who will challenge them nor will they place themselves in social settings where they are going to be collectively challenged. Examine the confusion that reigned when Trump kept going back to what was referred to as 'his base' and relatively rarely ever going beyond that concentric circle of 'support.' He was going back as much to 're-inflate' as he was to continue to propagate his alleged ideology. On February 17, 2017, Trump held an 'impromptu' rally (even though he was well into his first month as president). Again, the media coverage took the position that he was again, "*Going back to his base.*" And again, this not only dilutes how one of Trump's pathological ilk structurally operates, it also fails to understand the deeply inherent danger that is posed by what may best be understood as a communicable *psychological* virus.

Extrapolating the projective-identification of sociopathic narcissist to the sociopolitical understanding of Hegel's *Master-Slave Dialectic* (*Herrschaft und Knechtschaft*), (which is more properly translated from German as *Lordship and Bondage*) one can begin to decipher a more complex appraisal. In the devolution of the dialectic, the collective *surrogates* become mercenaries of a solicitous political ideologue(s) that ultimately involve what we may refer to as switch-selling. This is where their constellation of propositions are directed toward the *disenfranchised, desperate* or *greedy* and allege for example to 'take back' or 'bring forth' change (usually ill-defined and nonspecific, but always rage-laden and rage inducing) to a retrospective make-believe time or time set-forth in a foreordination of *prophecies.* Yet, neither can ever be reached, for the congregate or collective *en masse* can ultimately never be permitted to exist outside of the retrospective or foreordinated strife.

However, what does come to fruition, often too late, is that the alleged *deal* which is a derivative of the postulates of the projective-identification that is put forth by the ideologues is substituted with the longitudinal delivery of an inferior set of substrates, with a denial of access to formerly promised projections.

A constellation of ideologues are the ones who serve primarily as a masthead, accoutered with projective promises that "*You too can be like me,*" the *Lord.* And in their representation of the ones that they often times clandestinely serve as advocates for, the hawking of the verbal missives are characterized by purple prose—where the delivery becomes the message and the meaning is obscured by an excessive and often outlandish use of adjectives, adverbs and metaphors as well as untraceable declarations of theories based upon an ill-gotten distortion of facts.

Further, in addition to the purple prose, the oratory is bombastic and blistering, intended to shut down opposition and also to inflict damage. Eliciting not only a defensive posture but ultimately to induce impotence. This was characteristic of Fascist Germany. A careful reading of *Mein Kampf* reveals these strikingly similar dynamics as do the surviving speeches delivered by Adolph Hitler.

'*Eein volk, ein reich, ein* führer,' is not only applicable to Fascist Germany. Examine Trump's emissary, Stephen Miller, stating that Trump's "National security actions of the president will *not* be questioned."

This structural dynamic becomes apparent when one observes any attempts at systematic annihilation of forward intellection with an expressed desire to *stagnate the evolution* of ideas and behavior while willfully confounding the meaning of stagnation with liberation. As is historically demonstrated time and again with any form of despotism, a critical aspect to incorporate into our understanding is the necessity of destroying the current and historical order as well as a concentrating of power over the public and domestic domain into the hands of a few, while creating and maintaining a *trompe l'oeil* that there is a wider distribution of power and voice, which factually does not exist. Not to be redundant, however, the destruction of not only free flowing and free form thought is essential to the despotic devolution, as is a comprehensive understanding of how projective-identification is inherent in this process.

If the sociopathic narcissist engages with another or a group where they are challenged, they will often create an *illusion of interest*, in terms of what the other may be saying or expressing. The rational for this engagement is to reduce the threat that is being experienced within the context of the dynamic. It is this feigning or a posturing that disarms the other. When the other is disarmed the ascending threat experienced by the sociopathic narcissist descends, his experience of losing control is now thwarted. The *other* is bought off with an *appearance of genuineness* and even apparent *concern/understanding*. Denial, distortion and lying are *de rigueur* for a sociopathic narcissist to function in the world. There is *never* an apology, there is *never* guilt and there is *never* remorse. However, the sociopathic narcissist *just* doesn't deny, distort and lie for the sole purpose of denying, distorting and lying, rather they *utilize* these linguistic dissimulations to create confusion and therefore cause others to *question* their perceptual reality. If they were to apologize, experience guilt or remorse then the projective-identification dynamic would have *failed* and they would have to reclaim what they were no longer able to control.

The narcissistic injury that Trump appeared to manifest regarding the number of people at the inauguration is an obvious example. Clearly reality *dictates* that one photograph shows vastly more people at the 2009 inauguration of Barack Obama than it does at the Trump inauguration. However, this is simply too much of a narcissistic injury/insult for Trump to contain internally. Here he is, *the* 'TRUMP' and he was upstaged by a *"black man who is not really a citizen of the United States and was born in Kenya and who TRUMP had 'proof' that his Hawaiian Birth certificate had been altered and was phony..."*

Trump responds with tweets that question the veracity of the photos and declares that the photos *really* do show more on his side than on President Obama's side. This is not just a challenge but also an attempt to once again alter the perceptions of reality by setting up a scenario where one, in order to believe TRUMP, has to *set* aside *their* very perceptual reality. However, they are from a projective-identification not relying on *their* perceptions, which have for all practical purposes become psychically debilitated, but rather on the reality now defined by an *external source*, in this case, Trump.

Politics is, in the case of Trump, only a conduit to manifest his narcissistic born projective-identification. Trump in his attack on the media and a myriad of intelligence agencies again is not just attacking them, he is using his pulpit to influence and alter the others' perception of what those agencies present, via projective-identification. When the end comes for Trump and those associated with him and I believe he *will* ultimately self-defeat himself to the point of annihilation, he will first use the illusion of 'alternative-facts' as a way in pleading his case. He will also *quickly* abandon his solicitous surrogate mercenaries. And, should he not abandon them he will only maintain his *loyalty* to them in order to protect himself.

The sociopathic narcissist believes that they not only can but also have the right to exercise their imposition onto or into whoever they happen to desire at the time. Think of the Billy Bush tape and Trump's uncensored statements about "grabbing their pussies..." The other, in this case, his *victims*, "*are lucky to have their pussies grabbed by me, there are many pussies I wouldn't waste my time on.*"

The tweeting allows Trump a way of expressing his narcissist wounding without direct challenge. This is a way in which he is able to rapidly discharge his narcissistic rage. The tweeting also allows for a window of discovery as to how little ascension of narcissistically bound anxiety he is able to *intra*psychically contain. Additionally, it is a way of maintaining control over those who he has successfully engaged within his web of projective-identifications.

A sociopathic narcissist *has* to have a defined enemy—without this he is nothing, as the enemy is the *causative* agent for *his* oppression or of those by which he is declaring himself the champion of. *First* an enemy or enemies must be declared, think of the "*radical Islamic terrorists*" or the "*Mexican rapists*" or for that matter Barack Obama or Hillary Clinton, however, they will also almost always be amorphous—a collective body or race—culture, for Hitler, Jews and those *declared* "impure." *Secondly*, after the declaration, the enemy *must* be continually augmented—*alternative facts*—to continue with the ill-defining of those who are now *clearly* the enemy. *Third*, it is necessary to now *receive* narcissistic gratification from those collective projective bodies who identify with whoever the enemy is now defined as. With Trump's obsession with the vast numbers at the rallies and of those who support him it becomes relatively obvious that he relies on these numbers not just for *himself* per se but rather for his pandering *others* to ensure that they continue to provide him with the sociopathic narcissistic reflections necessary for him to continue to manifest his primitive and profound narcissistic replenishing; it becomes a discharge—recharge synergistic dynamic. Once the equation is broken down it is relatively easy to envision not only the primitiveness of an individual of this psychic structure but also the fragility and dangerousness.

Trump *will not* and *cannot* change. Any change manifest would be strictly self-serving and illusory. *Every* thought, word, action and deed runs through his psychologically pathological conduit. To ignore or remain ignorant of an understanding of how Trump's sociopathic narcissism factors into and drives who he is and what he does will not just continue to result in mystifying confusion, but also make countless others vulnerable to his longitudinal destructiveness.

He *does not* self-perceive vulnerabilities of *any* type—when he is confronted by anything that remotely resembles 'failure' it will be construed to be the 'fault' of what or whoever he can target. And, revenge of some form he will seek. He also knows that most events don't last long and that memories are relatively short, therefore he can build crisis upon crisis without ever having to be confronted by any one event or set of circumstances for very long.

One of the grave dangers of a sociopathic narcissist is that they are *highly* vulnerable to praise or what children call goading, which from a national security standpoint makes any country under the possession of a sociopathic narcissist highly vulnerable.

Once Trump begins to characteriologically *devolve*, and he will as threats increase, is when he will become exponentially more dangerous, most particularly with regard to bringing about military conflict as this would represent the 'ultimate' demonstration of his power and ability to exercise control.

A critical aspect of Trump's pathological narcissistic devolution will likely center around what will ultimately be collectively per-ceived as his failure to fulfill the projective-identifications. Once these projections in essence begin to 'vibrate' loose and Trump lacks a sufficient number of projective objects to satisfy what has proved to be an insatiable pathological need for narcissistic gratification he must then *prove* that he is ultimately powerful and dominate. His utilization of what are euphemistically termed 'conspiracy theories' will become increasingly important to support his internal delusional process while at the same time increasing his paranoia. *Succinctly, this is not 'indulging' in conspiracy theories it is however, a manifestation of a paranoid delusional process.* He *has* to find an *organized* constellation of 'ideas' that in essence support his pathology.

Further, in order to function within the depth of the primitiveness of his pathology he must be able to see who he is and what he does as *infallible.* There is much discussion about "…*is what he does a plan of action(?)"* with regard to his relentless vengeful rhetoric. The simple answer to this terribly naïve or perhaps ignorant question is "No." Trump is *psychologically terminal* and what we are witnessing is the fabric of his personality increasing tatter and manifest in a narcissistic delusional form. *Perhaps* we are also seeing a dementia process manifesting, however, regardless of the etiology at this point it is critical that he be removed from office. The only hesitation I have with regard to impeachment is that the line of succession of course is the Vice President who appears to be as religiously preoccupied as Trump is narcissistically bound.

What is most important to understand is that everyone, every man, every woman, every child is *nothing* more than collateral damage for Trump. There will be those who defend and deny against this statement, however they will also be equally as invested in their cherished denial when Trump calls for the nuclear codes. The congress has played chicken with Trump and is now faced with how they manage their own psychopathy—what collateral damage are *they* as individuals and as a collective body willing to individually and collectively sustain and manage psychically?

In an additional note, Trump does not, as most would interpret it, 'lie.' Rather, his misrepresentation of what would clearly be defined as factual is based upon his *internal* misrepresentation and distortion of reality. This also, again, not to belabor a point, is by definition psychotic and in this internal quagmire of distortion of reality is precisely what makes Trump too unstable and ultimately too dangerous to occupy the presidency of the United States. Regardless on one's political ilk Trump is not just dangerous to the stability of the United States, he is a clear, present and ever increasing danger to the world at large as we know it.

In summation, consistently presented in the media exchanges are discussions of Donald Trump's 'base' and 'going back to his base.' The political pundits espouse their analysis and in essence social diagnostics to opine on this or that but rarely, if ever, examine the psychopathological aspects of what and why DT's base responds to his rhetoric. In any political dynamic the clinical processes are essential to examine in order to not only understand but also to enhance ones critical discernment to be able to identify a patho-logical process that not only influences but also manipulates.

The rage that is observed at DT's 'rallies' is born out of a projec-tion of paranoia. Paranoia by definition attenuates the complexity of mindful thought which then yields a state of rage filled collective euphoria. Ultimately, the *desire* of DT during the rally experience is to ensure that *en masse* the aggregate narcissistic mirror does not desilver and the *ergänzt warden* remains constant.

DT does not go back to 'energize his base,' as naively gets reported but rather to narcissistically enrich himself when he perceives his projectively-identified reflection eroding.

This is accomplished, as has been extensively discussed previously through the psychic aqueduct of *projective-identification* and exploiting those individuals who manifest a complimentary *introjective-identifi-cation*. However the key to understanding this primitive psychody-namic is that the rage filled P-I that DT promulgates acts as a catalyst to the collective I-I, which potentiates the psychic kinetic energy which therefore increases the probability to reach its apex activation barrier and ultimately result in a cacophony of negative behaviors, i.e., violence becomes legitimized and the *risky-shift* becomes ac-tualized, as can be seen through the violence being perpetrated in DT's name. The resulting rate of reaction will correlate to the manifest rage that is encompassed in the projective-identification.

What has also been missing from the discussions is how DT's 'base' are also his ultimate victims. They represent collateral damage for DT, as his *one and only* interest is himself and anyone who func-tions within his orbit, potentially including his blood-related family members, exist within a constant threat of psychic immolation.

Mary, Mary Quite Contrary

There once was a woman named Mary who was somewhere in her middle years. From childhood, Mary had been a problem to be dealt with. Setting this on fire, torturing cats and peeing whenever and wherever the fancy struck her. Usually referred to as the psychopathic triad. She grew to be a resilient self-mutilator, her body being tattooed with plentiful, beefy scars, often resembling cuts made for *specific* operations performed by surgeons, which she would say were the result of having to have emergency surgery. She also was a resilient survivor of many serious suicide attempts, hangings, overdoses, one small caliber gunshot to the abdomen, wrist slashings. She had seen her psychotherapist for many years, clinical hour after clinical hour, the therapist would say, of "…Suffering through Mary's relentless torture of me." The psychotherapist's office was at one of the local hospitals, and, when Mary became too unnerving or suicidal, she could be walked down the hallway and admitted to the inpatient unit for a "…Much needed reprieve." Although the psychotherapist always maintained her contact with Mary while on the IPU, seeing her daily. The day Mary locked herself in the bathroom and slammed her head onto the toilet bowl particularly frustrated Mary's therapist, having to "…Beg Mary, who had jammed the lock, to come out and not do more damage to herself." Eventually Mary emerged, her face a bloody mess and having a couple of loose teeth. "I don't know what to do with you," Mary's psychotherapist would say to her. Medications accomplished very little, and mostly Mary would store them away for a later suicide attempt. Mary said she didn't know either, but never, except under her own "terms," did she ever want to cease her therapy with her psychotherapist, they had been through too much together, she would say. She was just recovering from a serious overdose, while on the IPU, having cheeked her medications for several weeks, when, having been lingering by the hospital IPU's locked door, made a bold dash when a staff member failed to adequately see who may be planning an 'escape.' An alarm sounded. Mary's therapist, having realized it was she who absconded, began chasing her down the long flights of stairs, being followed by other staff with security now having joined in tow. Mary made it to the bottom of the stairs and then made a mad run toward the parking garage, directly adjacent to the hospital. There, Mary ran around the turnstile, dodging oncoming cars, until she made it to the top of the garage. She waited for the pursuing entourage to meet her. When Mary's psychotherapist approached her, Mary stepped over the heavy gage wire that cordoned off the sudden drop off to the pavement below. A hand reached over the wire, Mary's hand, and then her therapist stepped forward to take that hand. The hands clasped together. Mary looked into her therapist's eyes that beckoned her to step back over the wire and in that moment of interchange, Mary opened her fingers and tumbled back, falling onto the unforgiving concrete. Mary's psychotherapist stood atop the concrete garage, transfixed by shock at Mary's lifeless, splayed body seven stories below. Many years later in supervision she would explore her mixed feelings at Mary's death as well as having served as a projective repository for Mary over however many years.

Much discussion is made of the 'ability of the patient' to be able to 'utilize' the psychotherapist. *However*, little is understood as to how treatment can falter and become terminal *if* the psychotherapist becomes in essence, '*too projectively full*' to any longer serve as a psychic receptacle for the patient. This also, at least potentially, highlights the importance of in depth and challenging ongoing clinical supervision, most certainly not like supervision depicted on the television show *The Sopranos*, where not only the psychotherapist but the supervisor, by proxy, served to make the lead character a more efficient and dangerous psychopath. Mary's psychotherapist struggled until her death with her conflicted thoughts and affects about her treatment with Mary. "She is better off dead and so am I," she would say or "What a miserable life she had and she made mine miserable to boot." But, then it was characteristically followed by her guilt at feeling relieved and at times an overwhelming desire to mutilate herself.

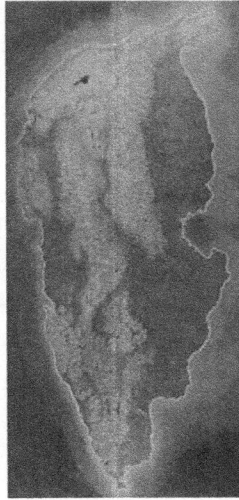

Wepdin

There was little to do now. His breathing was coming in short pants. A dam had broken in his lungs filling his air sacks with torrents of pus. An insidious tumor that innocuously began as a purplish dot on his nose exploded into a coup d'état successfully overthrowing his face. At this, the beginnings of the end, even the frontispiece of his silhouette looked like it had been splattered by a can of black eyed peas. His eyes were sunken into his bony skull, lost, roaming, what little strength that was left was spent holding the lids open wide, making the keratinization of conjunctiva eerily pronounced. Closer to the end he slept with his eyes taped open, the threatening permanent darkness looming like a drawn out game of chess with death. "*And when the Lamb had opened the seventh seal, there was silence in heaven about the space of half an hour.*" Day in, day out, this way and that, suffering through an indifferent God. Check; out of check, check; out of check… and on it went. It would take longer than thought to die. The nervous tried to assure him he would again pull through "…this bout"; he had to hold on for the coming cure, they would say.

Rev. Jerry Falwell announced that homosexuals are "Brute beasts," and that one day homo "sex u auls" will be "Utterly annihilated," and "Then, there will be a celebration in heaven." Ronald Reagan echoed his own sentiment stating that, "AIDS is the wrath of God on homosexuals." President Reagan and Rev. Falwell spent many hours commiserating about the Angel of Darkness bringing moral decay to the United States. God was now marching forth to seek his retribution.

When he had come into the hospital the first time he had been found naked and psychotic, running down the street frightening the sedate and sublime. Then, he was still a handsome man. No purple splotches covered his face and his testicles were of normal size. When he was admitted to the ward, he volunteered his diagnosis. Three years before, a few months after an encounter with someone who'd said he was "*safe,*" he came down with the worst flu of his life. There was so much talk then about getting 'the bug.'

He was their first. They'd always seen themselves as a sterile hospital, a religious institution where the staff was encouraged to pray with the patients. In addition to the cocktail of drugs to make him sane once again, he was also issued a blue armband. No other patient was to be within three feet of him and no staff was to touch him without gown, gloves and mask. Even then the nurse's hands trembled when he reached out to take his pills. He was a twentieth century leper.

In and out he would come and go over the next four years.

In his last year, there was no need for the arm band though, his diagnosis was unmistakable; he and *it* were indistinguishable. There were others coming now, beginning to dirty the hospitals doorstep. They just wouldn't stop showing up. Some not yet so thin; while others were gaunt with death's cowled head cresting like the sword of Damocles.

His arms on this day waved manically as they rolled him through the emergency room doors, like a supine preacher leading the choir in a hymn of redemption; His eyes blown out with desperation; his bloated belly ready to birth something that he never wanted to be pregnant with. His chitlined legs excruciatingly taut from the relentless third-spacing of the lymphatic fluid that now oozed through the cracked fissures that ran from his thighs to his feet. Once someone told him that he should die on his own terms, take control of his dying, "Die with dignity," they would say. *No matter the euphemisms, death is ugly.* He hadn't eaten in three days; in his final moments he would tell his father that at least he wouldn't shit himself at the end.

He had a Ph.D. in mathematics from New York University and spoke eleven languages fluently, *all* self-taught. So fluent he was in Portuguese that he worked his way through his doctorate serving as a translator at the U.N.

He'd never felt like he fit in anywhere, so goddamn smart he was. He did however enjoy kibitzing with other mathematicians in the faculty lounge nestled away on the top floor of the NYU mathematics building. It was here he found kinship in discussions on combinatorics, infinite series and set theory. One of his greatest moments was a day long discussion on classical analysis with Dr. Paul Erdos, who many consider, next to Archimedes, to be the greatest mathematician of all time. "Erdos was an oddball too," he would say.

His once full head of wavy dark brown almost black hair had wilted to a dry mangy wispiness. "Comfort measures only," his chart now said. A *'thank God that's not me'* smile was flashed by those who came into his room. Some of the morbidly curious, who'd never seen 'his kind' die, gowned up, came into his room and whispered quietly, their stouthearted faces cloaked behind blue surgical masks.

In November, 1967 his mother received a confusing call from a travel agent. "We have your husband's ticket reserved for Brazil," the agent said. His mother was accustomed to her husband traveling but he had not told her he was going to Brazil. He had founded a private telephone company and was always going here and there to sell this and that but *Brazil*, she thought to herself. When her husband answered the phone she said her feelings were hurt that he was traveling so far and to such an exotic place and had not at least asked her if she would like to go. "*What*, I'm not going to Brazil," was his response. It hit them both at the same time; *their son* was planning on going to Brazil. "Yes," he said when asked. He had made arrangements with the travel agent to travel to South America. "Just bill it to the company," he had told the travel agent. He was bored, he would say. He was ten now and thought it was time he got out on his own. "It's probably not a good idea to go to South America by yourself," his mother and father told him that night over dinner. Then they had to do something, he would retort, it was becoming too insufferably boring to go to school, come home, do homework, teach himself *Portuguese* and *Bahasa Indonesian*, eat supper, study plate tectonics, have a snack and go to bed.

On February first, 1983, one thousand twenty-five cases of AIDS was reported in the United States. Three hundred ninety-four had already died. By April 23, 1984, there were more than four thousand one hundred cases. Already one thousand eight hundred seven had died. The San Francisco health department alone reported more than five hundred cases.

The average heart beats about two point five billion beats in a lifetime. His would only get one billion three hundred sixty-three million two hundred fifty-nine thousand eight hundred eight times before stopping. He was shortchanged one billion one hundred thirty-six million seven hundred forty thousand one hundred ninety-two beats, give or take a few hundred thousand. Chemotherapy poisoning, cardiotoxicity; the destruction of the heart muscle. The initial damage occurs within one or two days of the first dose but the second wave of destruction and the most devastating happens a year or so later. The healthy beating heart sounds like Bach's *Three Partitas for Violin*; an elegant rhythmic, seemingly everlasting orchestration of life itself. But, chemotherapy is by definition a poison and as the course of treatment proceeds, killing the populating cancer cells, it also attacks the heart muscle like a Machiavellian mole.

The once well strung striations of the heart become slack and the once great Bach *Partita* devolves into a grade school ensemble. And then, the draw of the bow stops crossing the strings and we are no more. He would have but to endure just a few more hours of screeching.

Metal rings sliding around the stainless curtain rod rattled as the beige drape was pulled closed shrouding him from the everyday voyeurs. Every time someone who is dying comes into an ER there are onlookers. Voyeurism is rampant in hospitals especially for those deaths or diseases that are different from what most of us will die from. Right as a nurse was setting up his IV the squad arrived with a gunshot victim. A forty-five—year-old man had been sitting on his back porch, enjoying the sound of the birds and watching two blue jays fight over a bread crumb he had tossed into his yard. Several houses down another man, fed up with the squirrels eating his tomatoes, decided to take matters to another level. As his neighbor down the way sat and listened to the chirping, the fed-up man leveled a .22 rifle that he had not fired in twenty years out an open window, took a bead on one of the trouble-makers, and jerked the trigger. The small round nosed cartridge traveling at one thousand eighty Ft/s missed the pesky squirrel, ricocheted off this tree and that, finally slicing between the last two ribs of the resting neighbor, then tumbling end over end, tearing his liver to shreds, severing his hepatic artery. For a few seconds he felt a burning in his side, then, he lost consciousness, never to regain it again.

"Any surgeon in-house report to the ER—STAT, any surgeon in-house report to the ER—STAT," was broadcast over the loud speaker of the hospital. It was late in the afternoon on a Friday. Throughout the hospital only a plastic surgeon remained. When the surgeon cut open the mortally wounded neighbor's side any available pair of hands attempted to retract hamburgered liver tissue so the arterial geyser could be clamped off. Blood sprayed like an untamable spitting cobra. By the time the neighbor who had been minding his own business was pronounced dead, the room looked like the debris of a Rwandan massacre.

He was slipping in and out of consciousness now. His tissues, like starving refugees begging for food, saturated as much oxygen as they could from his sporadic breathing. Through his wilting voice he asked for someone to cover his face, knowing that others sensibilities were offended by his appearance. "I look worse than *Marla Hanson*," he would say.

On June 5th, 1986, just a few weeks after he was diagnosed, twenty-four year old model Marla Hanson, a striking brunette who lived at on West 34th Street, had, just a week before, rejected the unwanted sexual advances of her landlord, makeup artist Steven Roth. He continued to persist, making threats if she refused to acquiesce. "You are so goddamn fuckable," he would say to her. After all he was giving her a good deal on the apartment, only charging her six hundred dollars a month. She could return his generosity with a sexual favor.

The night before she'd called him and said she'd had enough of his menacing. A friend had offered her the sanctuary of a place where she could once again feel safe. As she left the next morning for a photo shoot, two thugs hired by Roth, right below the canopy of the apartment building, grabbed her. One held her in a full-nelson while the other sliced her face with a dermatome, severing the muscles that controlled her smile. Then he skinned her nose. The actress "*Divine*" was just coming out of the door of the apartment building as they were finishing with her. As best s/ he could, Divine fought off the thugs and cared for Hanson while waiting for the ambulance.

The wall that Divine's yellow-flowered couch sat against bordered Hanson's bedroom wall. On the other side of Hanson's living room wall was a fish tank filled with exotic fish, piles of books on theoretical mathematics and dictionaries from Portuguese, Spanish, German, French, Italian, Romanian, Russian, Farsi, Thai and Bengali. It was not uncommon for Hanson and Divine to hear *Mussorgsky's* opera, *Boris Godunov* echoing through the door as they walked to their apartments. Divine, Marla Hanson and the man with the aquarium fixed each other dinner when money was tight. They also had a running joke about

J. Edgar being "bad fruit." Sometimes, before she was brutalized, they would knock on Hanson's door and offer up a bowl of this or that, usually still steaming.

What does it mean to "…lapse into a coma?" This is what the

nurse's would say he was doing now. The ER physician glanced through the curtain, made his assessment from afar, ordered morphine and went about his way. He would soon be transferred up to a floor where he could die. An IV line ran from his left arm to a bag of saline hanging from a stainless steel rod with two Shirley Temple like curlicues twirling up on each end.

His eyes fluttered for a moment, only to give in again to the harbinger of the long sleep. Then he would jerk away from its grip and come back. During a lapse, a nurse had come in and put a catheter line into his penis. A dark brown fluid began seeping into the urine bag. The nurses talked about his face beyond the curtain, imagining that he was too far gone to hear what they were saying.

Patrick Buchanan, Communications Director for President Reagan, was making speeches declaring that, "AIDS is nature's revenge on gay men." Reagan didn't see any cause for alarm until fellow actor Rock Hudson announced that he was dying from AIDS. The president called Hudson in Paris where he was seeking treatment. But, Reagan did not mention AIDS publically for two years after Hudson's death.

In a long term care hospital a woman laid unresponsive for the past fifteen years. She was barely twenty when she was thrown head first through a car windshield. Her parents sat vigilante beside her bed, every day, waiting for God to gently touch her shoulder and rouse their daughter from her sleep, taking each muscle twitch or flutter of her eye lids as a sign of her eminent return to them. On another certain day, the hospital decided to move another comatose patient into her room. An emaciated young black man, whose brain was infused with the intracellular protozoan parasite *toxoplasma gondii*, which had infected him on a certain day, when he scooped cat shit from a litter box, creating a cloud of parasitically infused dust that insidiously filled his nose with hundreds of the hook shaped worms, that, in not too long of time, made their way to his brain. After being diagnosed with the *bug* the cat that he had taken in from the cold remained his only although ill-advised friend.

The young woman's parents were distraught that the abhorrently diseased young man, being one of them, would suddenly regain consciousness and rape their comatose daughter or that the AIDS virus might leap from his body to hers, putting her awakening at risk. This prompted the parents to file a complaint with the hospital board, who responded with an edict, that "Until further notice, any patient diagnosed with *acquired immune deficiency syndrome* shall be transferred to a more suitable facility."

Not that long after his parents had caught onto his scheme to start a new life in Brazil he began to think about *WEPDIN*. His mother and father, although loving and understanding, just couldn't bring themselves to let their ten-year-old son, precocious as he was, travel to Brazil—even if he *was* becoming fluent in Portuguese. Given that he would have to wait a while longer, he decided to begin "construction" of a place where his burning intellect could be forever sustained. In a dream he saw an island. Indonesian like, filled with culture and exotic foods, active volcanos and a people welcoming those who were different. It would also hold mysteries. Mysteries that would require a lifelong dedication to solving but that ultimately, like Escher's *Metamorphosis,* would have no solution.

He knew the four-color map conjecture would someday yield to a clever mathematicians mind. All of the great problems in mathematics would eventually fall. *He* after all had already worked through *How To Solve It* (1945, George Polya) twice and "without one sheet of paper," he would coyly say. But, *WEPDIN* would be would be *his* world, where, when a solution began lurking about, he only had to confound its unraveling by twisting it into a *Gordian Knot*. He began carrying about a soiled, torn canvas tote bag where he kept *WEPDIN's* evolving social traditions, language structure, economics and geothermal history. Later would come the flora and fauna.

Even though the nurses thought their pity of his face was camouflaged in their whispers, he heard every word. He was *going* but, "*I'm not gone yet,*" he said through a gurgle, rousing one last time to make his point known shortly before he died.

A few months after he had first been found naked and psychotic he spiked a fever and instead of breathing began wheezing. With each breath pains shot side to side through his chest, "…Like my ribs kept breaking over and over again." When he arrived at the emergency room that day they called him, "Mr. …" and told him he had *pneumocystis*. The fungus that caused it, *Pneumocystis jiroveci*, was everywhere. "We all carry it around inside of us," the doctor would say. But now his defenses were beginning to fail. Every what we "all carry around," would now become a sword of Damocles that continuously wavered just shy of his neck. The hydra had arrived and was now beginning to slowly eviscerate him. With each new trip to the hospital they began calling him "Mr. ..." less and less. Eventually he became a man with no name, only one who had this and that.

Surgeon General C. Everett Koop said in an interview that, "Gary Bauer [Reagan's chief advisor on domestic policy] ... was my nemesis in Washington because he kept me from the president. He kept me from the cabinet and he set up a wall of enmity between me and most of the people that surrounded Reagan because he believed that anybody who had AIDS ought to die with it."

He remembered fondly when his mother went to pick grape leaves from the vines of a local wine maker. She always rolled the leaves with such care. Rarely did one unravel. She roasted the pine nuts before rolling them into the rice, this was her secret, he would say. While he lay dying, his father remembered the *one* time he took him fishing. It was a small pond not far from their house where fathers would take their sons to show off their developing prowess as anglers. While his father was methodically explaining the nuances of casting, he was calculating the curve of the cast so as to place the worm, "Right in front of the fish's mouth." Unfortunately, the only mouth he hooked that day was his father's, landing the barb clean through his bottom lip. Tearfully his father would say on that final day, leaning over his bed, telling the story, that it didn't hurt nearly as much going in as it did coming out. It was his last fishing foray.

For torture to be effective the pain must be agonizing and spread out, unpredictable and most importantly, with no end in sight. This was how he came to know the purple dots as they began seemingly seeping together; the first dot of a fractal merging into a second dot, merging into a third dot, again and again and again; relentless in their pursuit of his face. His doctor said, "This *is* going to kill you, sooner rather than later, you may as well get used to the idea."

At the end he didn't know what he looked like, not having looked into a mirror for many months.

After his Brazilian misadventure *WEPDIN* became his lifelong obsession. Everything he did or pursued thereafter was with *WEPDIN* in mind. Even as a young boy he told his parents he wanted to be buried there. "It's where I want to go when I die," he would say. "It will be my Heaven." They would nervously pooh-pooh that kind of talk. Birthing a world was a massive undertaking, he joked that he knew what God must have gone through. He now had to create *WEPDIN*. First came drawings of the island. Its coastal perimeter would be similar to Australia. There would be four volcanos surrounded by dense tropical forests, lush with vegetation and exotic fruits. The cities would be vibrant, expansive, and yet, its people would always live under the looming threat of a Vesuvius like eruption.

He laid like a panting dog on the gurney. His back slightly elevated so as not to suffocate on the fluids beginning to pool here and there. When a word or two was able to pass over his lips it was coated with a dark yellow film of thick phlegm. Dozens of perfectly formed purple orbs now grew out of his gums; one had poised itself on the bottom of his tongue, shimming it against the roof of his mouth making his words sound swollen. He still wanted to say so much. He wasn't ready to stop talking.

"It is surprising that the President could remain silent as 6000 Americans died, that he could fail to acknowledge the epidemic's existence. Perhaps his staff felt he had to, since many of his New Right supporters have raised money by campaigning against homosexuals," Rep. Henry Waxman, 1985, first congressional hearing on the disease. So often the tide, when it does turn, turns only out of public outcry or an evolution of public attitude. Politicians rarely have a *'change of heart'* as is so often touted but rather a threat to their funding.

There wasn't much to do when it all started. Zidovudine (AZT) came along and quelled some of the virulence of the virus. Didanosine (DDI) and Zalcitabine (DDC) were added on a "compassionate basis"; a euphemism for helplessness. For a short while, AZT teased the afflicted with a temporary reprieve. Then, the lycanthropic virus, having seemed only to hide behind this organ or that, burst forth with a vengeance.

An unstoppable mole had infiltrated his body's immune system. The cunning viral foe began erasing his insides, taking a little of this, a bit more of that, until there would be nothing left but a hollow man. As his body became emptier and emptier, his death closed in on him more and more. Peter Freuchen wrote of being trapped in an arctic blizzard, the wailing of the wind competing with the wail of the hungry wolves, with both in hot pursuit. Freuchen in his tale decided to wait out the storm, building an igloo for shelter, the wolves leaping onto its top, trying to claw their way inside to the scent of fresh meat. Hour after hour went by until he began to realize that the walls of his shelter were increasingly closing in on him. Was he going insane? he asked himself. No, he would conclude, as he watched his warm breath freezing to the walls of the igloo, thickening them, exhale after exhale, increasingly making his ark of survival a frozen tomb. He was breathing himself to death.

As he lay dying, he dreamt that he was opening a jar of *Trotsky Cream*. He says, "It's important to remember what we have." It's too late; the cream had turned to dust.

He had just returned from the borderland between Brazil and Argentina, staying with this family and that, delighting in the sweaty swarthy men who found him *un atractivo gringo*.

The *Cataratas do Iguaçu quedas* drew him not only for their continuous roar and cascading beauty but also for their remoteness. Massive deforestation had not yet begun consuming the rainforest and the Guarani Indians were still in their thatched hut villages.

It wasn't long after he left that the hardhats came and did their work, bringing with them two heavy bladed bulldozers hooked together by a thick linked chain. They drove in parallel, ripping the one hundred sixty foot Brazilian nut trees out by their thousand year old roots and sending the Guarani hither and yon. It was here he was able to refine his Portuguese; to discover the nuances, the almost imperceptible inflections of the language. It was also here that a *mulher medicin* combined stevia leaves and licorice pepper had cured him of a high fever and delirium.

Shortly after he returned to New York, he saw an unusual ad for a "…personal Portuguese translator." "Some travel is required," the ad said. The voice on the phone told him to come to the interview right then, he was in dire need of someone who spoke *fluent* Portuguese. The voice also asked him how adept he was at reading faces, particularly in "…let's say *stressful* situations." He offered assurance to the voice. When he arrived at the address, he found a note taped to the door, directing him to another address. The cab fare would be taken care of once he arrived.

The stairwell that led to the "World Headquarters" was dank and smelled of sweet smoke. There was a dim bulb that hung from a frayed cord. When he got to the top of the stairs the door opened. He was greeted with "*Hey* man… come on in." The voice had on a white porkpie hat, shoulder-length hair and amber-tinted aviator sunglasses. Standing before him was Tom Forcade, the founder and editor of *High Times* magazine. The job involved flying to remote airfields in Brazil and picking up a load of marijuana. Forcade needed someone who spoke Portuguese to negotiate with the Brazilians *and* to let him know if they were about to be shot. Each trip would pay *ten thousand* in cash. They would fly back into a private landing strip in Texas, unload and then make their way back to New York City.

He made a total of five trips over the year. Most of the time it was in a Cessna 401 Twin with a gutted cabin. A few times Forcade piloted the plane, although he said he didn't have a pilot's license. Other times his bodyguard left-chaired. Regardless, the takeoffs and especially the landings were more terrifying than thugs with guns, demanding that the *maconha* be loaded *mais rápido* before the *Federales* came and took them all to the *Campo Grande, Mato Grosso do Sul*, the most notorious prison in all of South America.

Even though the Cessna could handle a large payload, sometimes there was so much *maconha* that the twin barely cleared the remnants of the chopped trees at the end of the grassy runway. Once they cleared U.S. airspace they flew as low as possible until they landed on a 'friendly' dry lake bed on a ranch just outside of Port Arthur, Texas. There the maconha was swapped for duffel bags of cash. He would be paid his ten thousand dollar fee before they landed again in New York.

After a year or so, he said he was done. Enough money had been saved up to put down on the West 34th Street apartment. *High Times* was flying now and Forcade had become a folk hero. They had departed friends. On November 18th, 1978 he found himself walking by Forcade's haunt. He'd heard that Forcade was trying to appear more legit and even had a secretary.

The door to the *High Times* office was cracked open and there, at a dilapidated desk, sat a disheveled bottled blonde, her head propped up by cupped hands, crying. "I am looking for Tom," he said. The blonde looked up through tear-caked mascara and said, "Tom shot himself in the head last night."

When the purple dots began growing together on his face, he hadn't yet realized that they had already rooted inside of him. It had been a Trojan horse, waiting for just the opportune moment to open its side, send seedlings scurrying down a ladder of DNA and begin defiling his blood rich organs. "We can treat you with Interferon-Alpha," his infectious disease specialist would say, but he'd then add, "but, it won't do any good."

"Maybe it was worth a try," he would say. Yes, it was going to kill him but not just then. Shortly thereafter he began a twenty-four week course of treatment. After the first couple of weeks his bones began to ache, little here, little there. His energy was becoming different too. A noticeable lack of peppiness. And each morning he would look into a mirror. "Yep, that one's getting smaller," he would say, sometimes out loud. Then, other times he would ask his parents if they noticed a selected spot retreating. "Yes," they would kindly say, "I think so." It took a few weeks before he abruptly shit himself.

He forced himself out of the house, going to a restaurant with another spotted friend. Sitting, chatting for the first time is weeks, nonchalant, waving a cigarette, animated, even for a moment laughing. Then an unexplained swelling in his belly erupted into explosive diarrhea, filling his chair and running out his pants leg. Screaming, mortified, he ran out of the restaurant, a trail of shit following him.

Hours afterward, everything seemed to go haywire. As sudden as the diarrhea came on so did constipation and bloating. Diarrhea again, this time with thick, black, tarry stools. "Where could the poop come from?" he would ask to no one, "I can't eat." Like the Pharaoh who demanded his slaves make bricks without straw, it seemed his body was making shit without food. Then, suppurating welts ballooned up from his skin, leaving sticky, yellow slug like trails wherever they ran. His breath kept getting shorter and shorter and now he couldn't pee. He would have to be catheterized. There was still fifteen more weeks of treatment left. Hanging on, hanging on, hanging on, shitting here and there, chills, bleeding gums and then it would begin again. And in between he would look in the mirror and say in a barely audible whisper, "I think that one's gotten smaller too."

He had moved back into his parents' upper middle class home, tucked behind tall topiary shrubs, in a well-manicured neighborhood. Only by necessity did anyone come to visit as they were now, by friends of many years, seen as harbingers of the Plague of Galen.

"Here, in addition to the conditions of the days of Noah, we have perversions of sex, including sodomy, homosexuality and lesbianism. Strange as it may seem, these movements have now come out in the open and are demanding recognition in society as legitimate and are being portrayed for us on the screen in the theater. Many people are turning to perversion," Anita Bryant, 1971, Apocalyptic Conference, Florida. He said that Bryant had had it up her ass once, didn't like it and that was what had ignited her rage. Then again, he would add with a smirk, maybe she *did* like it.

On the final day, he rolled through the ER, "No reason to keep him here," the physician said. And he was transferred on up to a room. It was kept dark for some reason, why, his eyes were closed. His father, his kind, dear father, leaned over his son, holding his hand, and kissed a face that he barely recognized as the face of his once handsome son. Ducted dripped tears followed the sulci of what had become his thick mallow protuberant death mask. One week to the day before his last day he came to my office one last time, propped by two canes. He undid his pants and let them fall to the floor. Pulling down his underwear revealed his penis being consumed by his massively swollen purple balls caused by the lymphedema caused by the consumptive and unrelenting Kaposi's.

With each step, he had to squat, and then push his legs out to the side, in order not to collapse in agony.

In his final hours his heart failed and failed and failed until there was nothing left to fail and its beat unceremoniously stopped.

He was cremated the following day and most of his ashes were scattered in the creek that ran behind the family home.

A few months before he died he completed *WEPDIN*. It resembled Australia in geographic proportions and had an active volcano, a rain forest and several vibrant cities. He had written its geopolitical and sociocultural history.

WEPDIN is twelve feet by five feet and is made of a specially compounded clay that he developed. He sculpted and painted every cubic centimeter much like God perhaps created what *He* wanted to be remembered for. There was a photograph of *WEPDIN* that hung behind my office chair that I took shortly after he "birthed it..." At that time I was seeing a patient who was a photo analyst for the CIA. On the afternoon that I hung the image she sat down across from me and became clearly distracted as she kept looking over my shoulder at the photograph. "I know *every* goddamn island on this earth, but *that* one, where the fuck is it?" she emphatically demanded.

On a particularly rainy day, at a small private memorial service, the few ashes that were saved from the flowing waters of the creek were carefully painted into *WEPDIN*, right where he had made the flatland end and the rainforest begin.

Thoughts, Observations and some Ranting and Raving

I would think that Hitler was pleasant sometimes, most especially when he was entranced by his own narcissistic bliss or unless of course you were Jewish or represented any other '*inferior* race, nationality or religion.'

One has to wonder what the final hour was like for Hitler and Eva Braun. What was the discussion that led to their suicides? What was the dialogue, the decisioning process? Was it that Hitler was in fact distraught over Benito Mussolini and his wife's murder only hours before and then the public degradation of their bodies? Or perhaps was it a narcissistic injury that was too great for him to internally manage: the loss of the war and Berlin being overrun by Soviet troops rapidly encroaching on the *Führerbunker*. Was Hitler seductive with Eva Braun to induce her to drink cyanide, was he directly forceful or was she so consumed by Hitler's projective-identifications that her death represented a double-suicide? Clearly one will never know and yet the idea that Hitler, like so many diabolical dictators, utilized Projective-Identification to control their subjugated cannot be overlooked. There is a consistent pattern of social control that we see being repeated by despots throughout history, with perhaps Hitler being the most cruelly efficient in his despotism. One characterological truism that we observe in individuals structured of this ilk is a lifelong history of pathological rage, both, in one form or another, at oneself as well as a defined constellation of a defined *enemy* that by the despot's projective focus is the causative agent for their and their resonate subjugated. One must first find a resonate population *source*. Typically one that is on the downtrodden. Economically depressed and psychologically vulnerable for one who will in essence pick them up and liberate them from their life of toil, misery and real or ideated victimization. The subjugated become emotional vessels for not only the projective message but also as a collective body to 'rally' forth in opposition to the now defined causative-agent(s) for their ills. Much is of course speculated by historians about his behavior, however little if any speculation is proffered with regard to the characterological catalysts for his behavior beyond the clichéd '...he had an abusive father, his mother was distant and unavailable, etc.' The collective field of psychiatry et al functions more like a sideshow shell game in an attempt to make up for our woeful ignorance about the human condition.

In briefly examining the psychological evaluation of John Hinkley, the would-be assassin who attempted to murder President Ronald Reagan, one can see how competing clinical ideas reach no conclusions that would result in any effective understanding of Mr. Hinkley's psychopathology.

The evaluations conclusions were that Mr. Hinkley suffered from: Axis I: Major Depression, recurrent, in partial remission; Axis II: Schizotypal Personality, Borderline Personality, Narcissistic Personality, and Schizoid Personality. In other words he suffered from a combinatorial and as of yet undefined constellations of personality disorders. The evaluation was conducted by *six* evaluators that reads with less clarity than *Finnegan's Wake*. This is not just an empty complaint, rather it must be considered within the context of how we conceptualize psychological structure and diagnoses. We must remember that Mr. Hinkley *was* the individual who shot the *President of the United States*. If this is the 'quality' of evaluation, by the nations "finest clinicians" that an individual of Mr. Hinkley's notoriety manifests, then what can some poor schlep expect from those clinicians who are at best barely trained beyond decision tree diagnostics or were admitted and granted diagnostic privileges through credit card admissions in countless masters and doctorate programs. I recall being in a seminar with one of the world's *pre-eminent psychoanalysts* whose Ph.D. is in English literature. It was posed during the seminar that the symptoms that were being presented with regard to intermittent outburst of rage may not be do, as was put forth as *fact*, to an unresolved oedipal conflict but may be associated with a reported motor vehicle accident and possible amygdalic seizures, whereby the patient went through the windshield and was comatose for more than a month before regaining consciousness. The response from the analyst was, "I don't think in those terms…" How can one *NOT* 'think in those terms' if one is consulting with an individual whose cause and effect etiology *mandates* examining for aberrations in behavior. This is most certainly NOT a mandate on promoting 'evidence-based' therapy, which as far as I have observed is cherry picked data to support our narcissistic need for validation and to counter our confrontation with clinical impotence. Rather, this is a perspective that when we are with a patient it is *required* that we structure the therapy, including diagnosis, to the patient and *NOT* attempt to vacuum seal the patient into a particular therapeutic paradigm.

Imaginary Sanity

A college professor of psychology (*Psychology 112* was the catalogue designation) many years ago swung his briefcase like a pendulum as he walked, seemingly not caring if another were on the upswing or the downswing. When walking a safe distance from him it was not uncommon to hear guttural sounds of his obliviousness. I recall vividly sitting in his experimental psychology class. The classroom was arranged in a way to where the professor's desk was pushed to the right of the door in a rectangled classroom. Sitting three seats back was a tall lanky fellow, looking like an untaut shoestring, who always seemed to have something about nothing to say. One afternoon in between destructuring a formula for the standard deviation, the lanky fellow pulled his briefcase up to his lap and proceeded to pull out a revolver. Sitting a few seats to the left of him the revolver looked like a blank starter's pistol. The professor, with his briefcase opened on his desk, proceeded to tell him to put the gun away. Which he did not and then had to be told again. Sitting directly beside the door was a fellow who happened to be a lineman for the local utility company, about six foot three and weighing in at about two hundred forty pounds. When the lanky fellow pulled out his pistol the third time the psychology professor became angry and told him to "...put it away or get out of class." The lanky fellow stood up, pointed the pistol at the psychology professor and pulled the trigger. The psychology professor's pressed white shirt turned red with blood and he was thrown into the black board. The classroom erupted with screams as the lanky fellow began leaping over other students and desks making his way to the door, the psychology professor now lying on the floor in a pool of blood. Right as the lanky murderer was about to breech the door the lineman took hold of him, spun him this way and that before slamming him into the blackboard erasing the chalky part where the standard deviation is derived from the variance. The lanky murderer hit the board hard as the lineman was atop him with his fist drawn ready to engage in justifiable homicide when suddenly the psychology professor leapt to his feet screaming, "STOP, STOP it was only an experiment...!" Fortunately the lineman's judgment was better than the psychology professor's and luckily for the would-be-lanky-murdering-student his *only* injury was a broken collar bone.

The class was enraged and after the screaming was quelled walked out en masse. What happened after that is a mystery. Class resumed a week later and the psychology professor said the experiment had been a failure and the students had not reacted as they were 'supposed' to according to the 'experimental protocol' he had established for the experiment. Everyone got an 'A' for the course. It was roughly ten years later when I accepted a position as clinical supervisor at a psychiatric hospital's satellite office. Part of our staff I learned were students from the local doctoral program in psychology. In a short while I met the students and much to my surprise was the college professor who had been 'shot' by the unfortunate lanky student.

It wasn't long before questions began to arise about his therapeutic approach with patients. It was decided by the doctoral program that perhaps a better placement could be found for him. One that allowed him to redirect his interest perhaps toward organizational psychology. But, first he must begin the process of transferring his patients to another clinician.

One patient in particular caused great disconsternation. Thelma, "...*When she arrived for her appointment today her long strawberry blonde hair cascaded down over her well-developed breasts that were revealed through her blue chiffon braless blouse. Thelma spent many years as a street walker...*" one of his clinical notes read. He could not be removed from the program he argued as he had "vastly more experience" than the other students having been a professor long before many of the students had been born. Plus later it was discovered he was the son-in-law of one of the largest financial supporters of the university. On his final day Thelma was scheduled for her final session. It would be a transfer session. Thelma came in that day wearing what was obviously her blue chiffon blouse that the former college professor had taken such a liking to and was in fact braless. Accompanying her was her long-standing boyfriend who it so happened had just been released from an extended stay in prison for *actual* attempted murder. The boyfriend was bald with the exception of the deep red veins that encircled his smooth skull and had trench marks on his face both from what appeared to be terminal acne and scars from shank fights in prison.

In the office the safest chair was clearly the one that sat closest to the door. The other three seating options were the chair at the desk and an arm chair that sat close to the couch. After a few minutes of seductive repartee between the former college professor and Thelma, her boyfriend began grunting, gripping the arms of the chair on which he sat. Thelma, with her chin resting between her 'voluptuous breasts,' looking needy, and upon raising her head, revealed her eyes wet with tears. This became too much for the former college professor to manage. And in his "loving manner" as the has-been professor would later describe his behavior to the police, he stood up, walked over and began caressing Thelma's face. Her boyfriend, having had enough, leapt to his feet and now, and without any mistaking, began making deep guttural grunts as he grabbed the former lovingly mannered college professor and slammed him into the wall. In a bizarre twist of fate, he broke his collar bone. Having been a prisoner on and off for most of his life, Thelma's boyfriend had the where-with-all not to go any further, meaning not to permanently maim the former college professor. He took Thelma's hand, and before he left, he also reached out and shook the hand of the person sitting close to the door, saying he was sorry that he had lost his temper but that Thelma had told him that she got tired of the former college professor turned "doctor" trying to touch her and had even asked if he could come over and have coffee with her after he left the office, he'd said he thought they could become "good friends." Her boyfriend wanted to see for himself but hadn't figured that the former college professor would be "stupid enough" to do anything with him there. "I guess I was wrong," her boyfriend said. The former college professor was lying in a huddle, moaning and bemoaning being attacked so "mercilessly." The secretary had heard the commotion and the guttural grunting and had called the sheriff who arrived right as Thelma and her boyfriend were leaving, hand in hand. They were detained and the former college professor said that he was providing "therapeutic comfort" when her boyfriend attacked him. Fortunately for the boyfriend there was another in the room who failed to corroborate the former college professor's recounting of the details of the event. The boyfriend would have gone back to prison for being goaded by the former college professor, Thelma would have likely gone back to 'street walking' *knowing* that in her experience men are in fact those who take advantage of women and hurt them in whatever manner they choose to express their psychopathy. But on that day, a man who clearly had countless struggles with his rage stood up for her and also chose not to leave her by murdering her offender.

The former college professor went from one intern setting to another, for the same type of misbehavior, finally graduating with 'a gentleman's agreement' that he would not practice 'clinically' and only seek professorial opportunities in industry or academia. A short while later, he opened his private office specializing in "*Counseling, For Those Forlorned By Love.*"

Note

One central aspect of reading, i.e., studying well-written and well-conceived clinical papers is to both sensitize and desensitize oneself to the insights proffered in those writings. Writings that challenge and do not offer *formulaic simplicity* for change, which is signified as becoming a different person through this and that, which results in a state of self-exaltedness, which is thus imagined to be a life without strife.

Writings that penetrate and create quakes in our thinking and cause our emotional tectonics to shift this way and that.

There is also a difference between clinical writings that teach and inform and those writings that are written for those seeking clichés and euphemisms as a way of approaching their clinical practice.

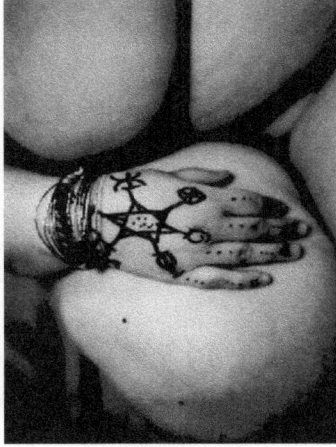

Being Exceptionally Odd

We are all odd. I've yet to meet someone who isn't. It seems that in many respects psychiatric diagnosis is more of a continuum of oddity. From A→Z there exists B→Y which would represent all of the permutations and combinations that exist between perfection and undefinable madness. With the advent of the DSMs we attempted to define more specifically what the B→Y's were. We didn't even bother with A and Z.

We used to diagnose men who fucked other men as a form of moderate madness, women who fucked other women were also considered moderately mad but the fantasy of two women together stimulated men more so they weren't quite as mad unless of course *they* happened to look like a man then it became harder to declare them *just* moderately mad. As the newest versions of the *Diagnostic and Statistical Manual of the American Psychiatric Association*, appear, they incorporate the most recently 'defined' parameters of madness that includes just about any aberration of behavior or thought we have yet to conjure up. Of course, as times goes on, and more variations of B→Y emerge then the DSMs∞ will *'protect'* us by ensuring that we are able to identify those *au courant* aberrations in the evolution of our insanity. Perhaps when alien life is finally revealed we will have to include *them* in our characterizations as they begin to come to us for treatment or *perhaps* us to them.

I remember now just about fifty years ago being an intern at a state hospital. Walking down the hall was a psychiatrist with limited ability to speak English, beside him was a woman diagnosed as *hebephrenic schizophrenic*. She was named Rosy, adorned in her three dresses, two or three coats, lipstick that she wore more like rouge and her hair forever a tossle. The psychiatrist was carrying a text book open to a certain page, pointing to a paragraph *screaming* to Rosy, "*OO dis, OO dis.*" And then, Rosy, so appreciative of *finally,* after so many years of being undefined and now *finally* being defined in her years of institutionalization, reached over and kissed him, leaving the imprint of her bright red lips on his cheek. Then she ran off as did the psychiatrist.

A short time later, Rosy, who had a penchant for stuffing toilet paper rolls as far down the toilets as her arm would reach, had just finished blocking up several poop portals when an out of house plumber arrived to cure the problem. The facility had two doors that allowed entry to the unit. In between each door was a short hallway where, should one of the mad one's attempt to escape, he would be captured between the doors that led from the world of defined madness to the door that led to the world of undefined madness.

The plumber entered the first door, carrying in each hand the tools of his trade. Upon reaching the second door he peered through the wire infused glass seeing those infused with insanity doing what those who are mad do: talking to themselves, rocking back and forth, pacing, screaming, shuffling, consumed by akathisia and masturbating ever so openly. The plumber buzzed and said he was there to unplug the plumbing and requested entrance onto the unit.

Rosy was at the opposite end of the hallway. Upon hearing the intercom call from the plumber she began running, her several layered coats competing for airspace as she sped down the hallway toward to plumber. As fate would have it, Rosy and the plumber encountered the same place in space at the exact same time. The plumber, in those seconds before their encounter, stood frozen as he saw Rosy careening past one representation of insanity after another until finally Rosy was upon him, literally. In that moment when the plumber and Rosy encountered each other Rosy leapt in the air, wrapped her legs around the plumber's waist and began madly kissing him. The plumber, having never encountered such a flagrant display of out and out lunacy, fell into unconsciousness, hitting the ground with a discernable thump. Rosy, sitting atop him, began moving her hips back and forth either riding him like a pony or a lust-filled lover.

The plumber recovered after being dosed with smelling salts, *quickly* went about his task of unclogging the toilets and then left, not even pausing to look back at Rosy who was waving as she watched him disappear through the wired glass as though he had not been there in the first place. Not long after that Rosy was given a lobotomy for her own good.

She showed up at my office one afternoon, standing outside my door with two large suitcases, saying she wanted to schedule an appointment. It had happened only a few times before, that someone who desired an appointment had literally knocked on my door, but never on those rare occasions had they been carrying suitcases. When I asked for her address she only said she was new to the city and still looking for a place to stay and that she was unemployed. However, she said with assurance, "I can afford to pay you." The appointment was scheduled for a week out. She promptly showed up for her appointment, again with her suitcases.

She was wanting to be seen multiple times per week as she was in the process of coming to terms with how she chose men as mates who were, "… unusual, usually anyway." She was on the run she said. Her husband, to whom she had been married for only about three years, was a funeral director. "Very successful" was he, she added. But, she had trouble given his success, understanding why he only conducted five or six funerals a year and then it seemed that all of the same mourners turned out for each and every service. Odd, she thought. And then there were the calls in the middle of the night, being awakened from a sound sleep, and her husband answering the phone, saying, "I'll be right there." Kissing her on the cheek and offering, "I've got to go get a body." Off he would go in his hearse. A few hours later his hearse would return and then not long after the roaring sound of the crematorium erupted.

He didn't have a bank account, "I don't trust fucking banks," he'd grumble. She was never allowed in the casket show room or the embalming area, he told her right after she had moved into the living quarters of the funeral home. "It would be too disturbing for you," he'd instruct. Then, one night after a few years, and right after a call came in to pick up a body and right after he told her it was going to take longer than usual, she decided to see how 'upset' she would become by seeing whatever she wasn't supposed to see.

Upon entering the casket show room, she saw dozens of caskets, from small to large, bronze, gray, copper and beautiful dark carved wood. She said she walked over to one of the more ornate oak coffins and tried to lift the lid. It was locked. But, hanging right above the light switch as you entered the room, was an L-shaped burnished casket key, resembling an Allen wrench with a handle. She took the key, slipped it into the small hole at the dead center of the casket and turned. There was a discernable *click* as the key tripped off the lock mechanism. Then she pushed open the lid and gasped out loud as she, as her husband had predicted, was thunderstruck.

The oak box was stuffed with money. Hundreds of thousands of dollars. She then went to each casket and looked inside. Each one was filled with money, ultimately she estimated, "millions of dollars." Later she figured that he was an "...undertaker for the mob." And, she also figured that someday he would for whatever reason decide that she was no longer useful to him and she too would suffer the fate of the crematoria flames. So, over the next few weeks she made her plans, organizing a drawer with exactly what she needed to make a quick getaway, a few photos and a bus ticket. Then, after her plans were secure, and on the night that the last call she would be awoken by came to the phone beside their bed, awaiting an hour or so after he had left, she quickly went about collecting what she had strategically placed here and there in preparation for her exit.

She lifted the two heavy suitcases into the trunk of the car he had allowed her to use and headed into the city. Then she parked the car a mile or so away from the bus station, lugged her suitcases to the ticket window, bought a bus ticket and waited. A few hours later her bus arrived. The bus driver tossed her suitcases into the hold and off they went. Thirty-some hours later and several transfers from this to that bus she arrived at where she was going. Then she spent another twenty or so hours on another bus to ensure that her tracks would be ever hard to follow. Before she left and to "Ensure my future," she said, she went to the casket room, popped the top of the oak casket and helped herself to five hundred thousand dollars, two hundred fifty thousand in each suitcase. "It was my alimony," she declared. She lived in an area where she didn't need a car, had no credit, clearly she didn't need any and kept to herself. It wasn't long after that, needing some companionship, that she met another man, considerably younger than she was and who only had one arm. It seemed that when the draft had rolled up his number he decided it would be better to cut off his arm than to go to Vietnam. So he laid his arm across a railroad track, having pre-*tourniqueted* it and let a freight train sever it right above his elbow.

The relationship didn't last very long as he didn't want to pay for anything and kept hounding her as to how she lived, having no visible means of support. The last I heard she went back to school to become a therapist, working with women who were wanting to as she liked to say, "...reestablish themselves." Each and every session, she would open one of her suitcases, count out my fee and then be on her way.

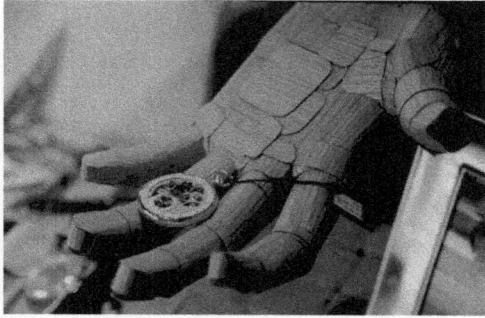

Some Thoughts About Some Couples Over The Years

Several things have stood out with regard to how couples seem to survive and thrive over the long haul of a relationship. These are not meant to be thought of as clichés as all of these dynamics are replete with power struggles and issues of control and dominance which feed and exacerbate all that is and is not held dear within the context of any relationship.

Relationships are *not* as many self-help books promulgate, 50/50. They are however, even in the worse of circumstances, 100/100. In order for a relationship to be successful, even the tortuous ones, each partner must be in essence *all in*. But, how we define success is a conundrum.

Successful relationships are typically thought of as *pretty*, not in a physical sense but rather as ones that do not air their differences in a public forum or ones that are held up (projected) by others to be exemplary. However, a successful relationship also can mean one where the couple is dedicated to not only the destruction of the relationship but also to the destruction of each other. A marriage can be a form of emotional suicide (as well as physical) whereby each member of the dyad becomes involved with the other to ensure their own emotional demise or at the very least their intractability to grow beyond their stagnated developmental positions. How couples describe their relationships behind closed doors is where validity lies not that which is projected exhibitionisticly in a public forum.

In a relationship, one doesn't come to a conclusion by being *right*. You come to a conclusion by compromise and understanding. To be obsessed with being *right* is an alternative way of disengaging from not only one's partner but also being ill concerned about the relationship itself and therefore willing to sacrifice the relationship for a momentary narcissistic gratification of dominance. A focus on being *right* also precludes being engaged with the other through listening as when ones focus is on establishing *rightness*, then, one has to prepare their response before the other is finished with what they were saying. Being *right* also sets forth a form of paranoia as the *right* partner has to actively listen for opportunities to *correct* the *wrong* partner or others. *Facts* become minutiae, extrapolations of meaningless fodder to be used as proof of one's *rightness* to the other's *wrongness*. Called for examples during the strifefull engagements are not opportunities for establishing mutuality but rather as opportunities for a '*specific*' disavow of the '*facts*' whereas lying takes the form of a more palatable constellation of denials. Only through compromise, compassion and nonthreatening confrontation does furthering of the relationship occur in a growth enhancing manner.

In a growth enhancing relationship there is a deep and abiding dedication to protecting the intimacy between the parties. Undoing emotional safety is understood to be just as violate as unfaithfulness and betrayal.

The excitement of the newness of a developing relationship evolves into an intensity of the intimacy and a *dedication* to each other's well-being.

Relationships die a hard death when the parties begin to identify each other as the enemy. Hounding one another is a sign of a loss of trust and signals that one can only count on the other to disappoint.

Blood-letting comments leave thick emotional scars that create psychic barriers and suspicion when a comment of tenderness *is* expressed. A comment born of tenderness is thus heard and experienced as a lie to the counter of the blood-letting comment.

Most often the blood–letting comment creates an affective lesion, one that erodes away over time the possibility for deep emotional penetration of counter-erosive comments. The opposite comments now have to move through the scar tissue to be not only heard but *experienced* without mistrust. Over time the scars thicken increasing their intensity thus further inhibiting the ability to express intimacy without questioning every move or gesture and ultimately any attempt at disinhibited relating.

A disrobing once enveloped in pleasure becomes tortuous exhibitionism in the literal face of an expected or remembered emotional lashing. One way or another these are unrecoverable declarations that result in the longitudinal deterioration of a relationship's intimacy.

There are projections of therapists and clinical schools of thought whereby if a couple does this or that miraculous intervention that there will be a softening or stretching of the corrosive scar, making the associated pain less trenchant. But, like an emotionally noisome tattoo that has been 'covered–up' with another more appealing emblematic placation, the old ink, like the old emotions, leaches through.

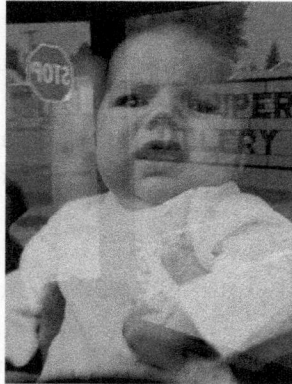

Inflection and Intonation

In movies one can tell when there is about to be a devolution of the plot or the character when the background music goes from a major key to a minor key. For our discussion we will consider

Inflection as the physical aspects of the speech sounds that serves to represent in essence a drop from a major to a minor key, as that which carries the *affective* representation of the speech sounds and how these manifestations of language are both projected and interpreted by the therapist and the patient.

Patients are exquisitely sensitive to how what they say flows *through* the therapist and then thusly back out via interpretation or insight-related comments. More often than not, particularly in the case of those therapists who have not spent time dedicated to their own treatment, the patient is often more sensitive than the clinician. For example, a therapist, whose *modus operandi* is to respond to most statements with, "Ummmm, ummmmm..." with a look of deep concern and a thumb on their chin, seems on the surface to offer a supportive understanding of what the patient is saying and experiencing. However, the therapist in this example offers nothing of themselves, not in essence giving anything beyond what *appears* to be a perfunctory laden response. There of course is the argument that this is enough. But, what may also be at play is a patient who does not seek more and the "Ummmm's" allow for what amounts to permission to remain the same without challenging what the patient is presenting. In a narcissistic therapist, the "Ummmm's" and alleged deep understanding can quickly devolve into a deep sigh and raised eye brow when it is revealed that the therapist's 'advice' was *disvalued* by not being taken and the patient made a decision outside of the therapist's proffered *wisdom*.

What may be best understood here is that to engage in an ongoing therapeutic dynamic the therapist must be able to listen beyond his or her own censoring. The material that the patient presents must be able to invoke the depths of the unconscious that can be presented either directly or in metaphoric form. The 'famous' response of Theodor Reik, when a female patient noticed a book on his shelf that was upside down, "...Why didn't you tell me you had had an abortion" is clearly within the realm of what I am referring to. Frederick Perls, who was by any measure his own worst enemy, was brilliant at being able to *see* that which lay at the core where psychological healing takes place. Howard Fink, a therapist of extraordinary brilliance and a protégé of Perls, listened with such a depth of intensity that many who went to him were intimidated by his presence. Fink often talked about his training with Milton Erickson, whereby Erickson spoke of the importance of '*opening the seven doors.*' Being able to 'speak to someone on at seven different levels at the same time, sometimes at the same minute.' Fink would say this was one of the hallmarks of a *deep* respectful attentiveness and concern. He also said that he believed that it was important to be able to 'articulate' the seven levels but that he also believed that it was more important to be able to feel those 'levels.' It is also critically important to have an unreserved and dangerous belief in the unconscious.

I remember a young man I saw many years ago. His father had been a psychologist of some renown. By all accounts a good man. One day the father began to complain of an intense headache on the left side of his head. Fierce, unrelenting and then sudden-ly debilitating. He was taken to the emergency room where an x-ray revealed a tumor sitting on the left side of his head. Later it would be diagnosed as a *Glomus Jugulare*. Rare but by definition benign. The problem with many benign brain tumors is that they grow back. This particular brain tumor was a monster wrapping its tentacles around this and that anatomical structures and most especially in 'Rob's' father's case, his brain stem. He lived but a few days after being admitted to intensive care from the ER. Neurosurgery was attempted but the 'sonofabitching' tumor was killing him and there was no way to stop it. To kill the tumor was to kill the host, which is what the family decided to do, when they "pulled the plug."

The tumor was known to be 'just benign' and not known to have an *RNA familial transmission pattern* until this particular time, when the genetics were just right and a few years after his father died, Rob began to have headaches.

Rob was a man plagued with a troubled past long before the tumor had its way with him. He'd killed a girl when he was just a teenager and driving profoundly drunk. The young girl was thrown from the back of the car when he hit a tree and died at the scene.

Later he would remember that somehow the back window of the car had nearly sheared her head off.

He became a profound alcoholic and highly dependent on marijuana. After he was diagnosed with the same tumor as his father, his notoriety came in the form of being written up in medical journals as "...Tumor X51...." His neurosurgery, which unlike his father's he survived, left him with a constant tearing and a blunted affect, plus a deep and abiding depression. He was his tumor and his tumor was he. Rob's body had been snatched and cloned by his tumor. Rational therapy was a useless endeavor which he described at length from the many years he had spent in some form of cognitive-based treatment.

One afternoon shortly after Rob had, in his deactivated way, related how he had come to be the way he was, he came into my office carrying a comic book. He laid it on his lap and said, "I just brought something to read because I knew I was going to be a bit early." I asked Rob to show me the cover. The title of the comic was *CYBORG*. Sitting for a minute, I saw CYBORG backwards and said, "*G Rob Y C*." Or perhaps better translated, "*Gee Rob Why See*?" At that point he began crying. There was nothing by definition 'rational' when I saw the deconstruction of CYBORG backwards and how Rob had in essence brought the comic book in not only for him to *see* but for me to *see* also. Rob had to choose that particular comic, to bring it into my office and to prominently lay it on his lap for me to see. It served as a conduit to the reciprocity of our unconscious, a way of Rob asking, perhaps begging to be *seen*, in whatever form that may have taken beyond "...Tumor X51...." It was a significant turn in his therapeutic journey. In my conception of psychotherapy, it is critical to listen beyond what is now often referred to as a patient's 'story.' Figure that the 'story' is double-spaced and what lies in between those double-spaced, interstitial 'blank' psychic intervals is the unconscious. And that 'blank' interval will give the therapist a greater depth to understanding and hearing not only what is 'going on' in our patients' lives but also too who they are beyond their stated and often shrouded words.

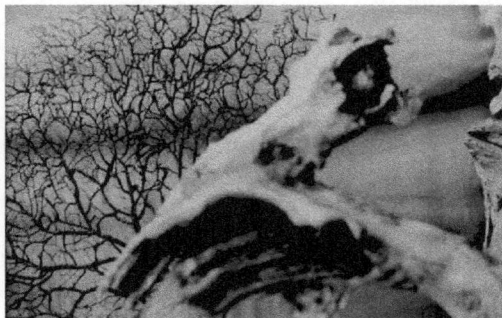

Presentation review of clinical documentary

A documentary was presented of a large, high-volume inpatient psychiatric teaching hospital. The following is a critical analysis of the *presented* interactions between two of the patients and both a psychiatric resident, *Dr. Clark* and his supervising psychiatrist, *Dr. Draper.* The two patients courted throughout the interchanges are *Sherry* and *Angel.* Sherry is paranoid schizophrenic, obese and has the characteristic appearance of someone who has struggled with schizophrenia for many years, including living on the edge and barely having enough to get by. Most certainly *not* someone who would likely be presented for an advertisement for the newest and *bestest* antipsychotic medication. Sherry is floridly psychotic at times in the production and wears glasses that are taped together at the temples, making her disheveled appearance even more dramatic.

Angel, by contrast, should she be seen walking down the street, would fail to raise any anxiety regarding her mental state. She is 'pretty' and wears a stylish black leather jacket which she constantly tries to get Sherry to "*wear.*"

At one point in the documentary Angel has done something that has resulted in Sherry 'getting into trouble.' The details of the resultant dynamics are not included in the production, however what is presented and is of significance is the interaction that occurs between Sherry, Angel and Dr. Clark.

In this interaction in the documentary, Sherry expresses her unwillingness to 'make-up' with Angel and Dr. Clark's attempted intervention to facilitate the 'make-up' between Sherry and Angel (the complete dialogue is presented in quotes).

Sherry: "I can't make up."

Dr. Clark: "Yes you can."

In this dynamic Dr. Clark not only ignores Sherry with regard to what she is expressing what she wants, he is also, by doing so, disavowing in point of fact her verisimilitude. He is in essence expressing his willingness to sacrifice Sherry's needs and desire for Angel's. Note that Dr. Clark's "Yes..." is not followed by an inflective comma, as his statement was demonstrative and made as a directive rather than something for Sherry to consider as an individuated decision.

Sherry: "I don't want to make up with her, because she got me into trouble."

Sherry then attempts to clarify her rationale for not wanting to "make-up" with Angel. Her statement is a clear and definitive declaration with no expressed ambiguity.

Dr. Clark: "You're a forgiving person." (Framed affectively as an empathic admonishment.)

One may on first examination consider this statement by Dr. Clark as a projection, however, his missive may more definitively serve to drive Sherry more mad and therefore make her perceptions less credible as ultimately, "You're a forgiving person..." has no definable meaning. Further, should one attempt to interpret it from a Judeo-Christian perspective, then it would also act as a Mobius strip, not only in denying that Sherry had no right NOT to forgive Angel but that should she continue to be a 'non-forgiving person' then she would suffer the fate of one who is non-forgiving, whatever the implied ambiguous meaning of that is. Continuing...

Sherry: "Not when I'm tied down and thrown in a..." Then Angel walks over, wraps her arms around Sherry and kisses her, while Dr. Clark stands silently and watches. *Clearly both Dr. Clark and Angel would have been aware of what had happened to Sherry, as a result of the past interaction with Angel. Obviously Sherry was restrained and placed (educated conjecture) in isolation. It however begs the question as to why Angel did (apparently) not suffer the same fate as Sherry? Thus increasing the resentment of Sherry toward Angel. Then as is observed in the documentary, Angel, without any intervention via Dr. Clark, kisses Sherry, who bristles at the touch of Angel but demonstrates marked restraint at this obvious unwanted intrusion.*

Dr. Clark: "That was a long time ago, *we're* going to have to forget about that and work on now."

Again Dr. Clark witnesses without intervening or even attempting to at the very least acknowledge Angel's boundary violating behavior. Therefore in his ignoring Angel's behavior he has legitimized and colluded with her, both in his silence and in his admonishment of Sherry for her failing to be a "forgiving person." Further, in Dr. Clark's stating "… That was a long time ago," he imposes <u>his</u> referential association of the event that Sherry is referring to overriding <u>hers</u>, which for Sherry clearly still exists in the present, observable moment.

Dr. Clark denies Sherry's associative memory regarding the consequences that resulted in her being restrained.

After Angel kisses Sherry on the cheek, Sherry then, with no obvious Segway, confronts Dr. Clark.

Sherry: "And you think she's so pretty and you want to seduce her, don't you?"

Dr. Clark: "No I don't, I don't think you should be concerned with *her*, you need to be concerned with you, okay?"

In the previous dynamic Dr. Clark has in his denial of Sherry's affective associations discredited her perceptions. In this confrontation, Dr. Clark is confronted by Sherry by what she perceives as his seductive behavior toward Angel. It is critically important to observe that Dr. Clark says in retort to Sherry's confrontation, "… No I don't" (Denial not only of perceptions but also of Sherry's reality) *and "I don't think you should be concerned with HER, you need to be concerned with you, <u>okay</u>?" In FACT Sherry is NOT manifesting "concern" with Angel in this interchange but rather directly with Dr. Clark's behavior toward Angel. However, Dr. Clark, while having the opportunity to disambiguate and acknowledge Sherry's reality testing, further compromises Sherry's reality testing by introducing even greater ambiguity. Further, "I don't think you should be concerned with HER, you need to be concerned with you, okay?" The "… okay" at the end of the statement appears to shift the statement from a sentence to an interrogative when in fact it is a <u>directive</u>. This by definition could be euphemistically called 'crazy making.'*

Sherry: "You have the hots for her and everything."

Dr. Clark: "I don't have the hots for anybody."

In one more attempt to confront Dr. Clark, Sherry goes on to address his behavior again. Now, Dr. Clark takes a global position of annihilating any possibility that Sherry's perceptions could have any gravity to them, by making an encyclopedic declaration that he is asexual. Dr. Clark leaves Sherry with nowhere to go in her desperate attempts to achieve some acknowledgement of her perceptual reality.

Many years ago I knew a psychotherapist who was married to another psychotherapist. Both were outstanding therapists and of great professional renown. When they were in their seventies she turned to him one night in bed and asked, "Are you having an affair?" Initially his first instinct was to deny what she was asking. However, he then said, "Yes." Later he said the reason that he acknowledged what she was asking was so he would not have to place his wife in a position where she would begin to question *her* reality with his denial for what she rightfully experienced as a shift in his relating and affectivity. Dr. Sheldon Kopp used to say that when a patient confronted him on something his immediate response was to acknowledge the confrontation and then he and the patient would talk about the fruitfulness of the confrontation. This way the patient not only would feel safe confronting him, but also that their reality testing and dignity would be preserved.

Let us explore further the interactions between Dr. Clark and Sherry.

After the snippet of interactions described previously the documentary moves to another exchange between Dr. Clark and Sherry.

Dr. Clark: "How's it going here?"

Sherry: "I don't know, sometimes—I don't trust you, sometimes I don't feel like _you_ come back and talk to me *and* _my_ anxiety."

Dr. Clark: "I don't come back and talk to you every day though?"

Again, in this dynamic interchange, Dr. Clark continues to refuse to acknowledge or respond to Sherry's basic perceptions about him. In Dr. Clark's presence, Sherry's objective reality is nullified by Dr. Clark's continued refusal to acknowledge her most basic perceptions and emotions about him. He *disassociates* himself from her while at the same time presents a psychic mirage of being someone who is not only interested in her but also the embodiment of someone who *cares*. Yet when Sherry reaches out to make contact *with* Dr. Clark, she finds herself grasping at smoke. Sherry clearly states she does not trust Dr. Clark. And in this exchange Sherry has little options except, in the continued presence of the denial by Dr. Clark, to deny her own reality.

The exchange continues:

Sherry: "I don't remember."

Dr. Clark: "So it makes you nervous?"

Sherry: "I wash the pills down my drain, talking helps to relate more. Washing the pills down the drain helps the system, but talking helps to relate more." In many respects it may be considered that Sherry is attempting to *preserve* her reality testing by not taking what could be reasonable speculated to be antipsychotic medication.

Dr. Clark: "Um hum. Does it feel good when _we_ talk to you?"

Sherry: "Yes, but I don't know how to live with myself."

Dr. Clark: "Do you like to talk, you're learning aren't you?"

Sherry: Crying...

In this exchange Sherry has stated that *Dr. Clark* does not come and talk with her. She is affectively expressing a sense of isolation and a desire to talk. However, Dr. Clark again does not respond to Sherry with regard to *their* interactions or his part in the didactic dynamic. Rather, he changes Sherry's confrontation that *he* does not come and talk with her to the collective "*we.*" Also, in his tagging his statement with, "…you're learning aren't you?" It must be considered whether Dr. Clark is implying through a statement affectively generated as an apparent interrogative that Sherry is 'learning how to talk,' *or* learning from their interactions that 'talking' results in a disavowing state of psychic impotence.

The dialogue continues.

Dr. Clark: "I'm going to work on the medication. Right? Very important, we're going to increase your Paxil, take 40 yea, that's gonna help, we're going to give you Orap, that's for the voices and that's for the thoughts. Okay and we'll give you Klonopin."

In the following exchange, Dr. Clark and Sherry are sitting at a conference table with two other staff members.

Sherry: "I'm in a lot of pain—there's nothing anybody can do for me."

Dr. Clark: "We're going to help you with the medication and you're going to help yourself." (As noted in the introduction Sherry's glasses are taped at the bridge and on one temple.)

"Alright," Dr. Clark is smiling, "take off your glasses."

Sherry: "Oh God, I'm scared."

Dr. Clark: "Why are you scared?"

Sherry: "I don't know what the hell is going to happen."

Dr. Clark hands Sherry a new pair of glasses and says, "This is a special case too. The newest style, huh?"

Sherry puts the glasses on—"Thank you Doctor." The staff seated at the table are clapping.

Dr. Clark: "How do they feel?"

Sherry: "They feel good."

Dr. Clark: "You're welcome. Now I can get rid of these." Dr. Clark takes Sherry's old glasses.

Sherry: "No!"

Dr. Clark: Holds up Sherry's taped up glasses. "Look at these things—come on, we can't throw these away? Let's throw these away like this is the old you. This is the old you *we don't want anymore*—and these glasses are going to represent the new you."

Sherry is only acceptable to Dr. Clark through *his* vision of her. *The glasses have become the personification of the culmination of the metaphoric representation of how Dr. Clark has consistently envisaged Sherry.* The *old* Sherry is *before* Dr. Clark (BC) while the *new* Sherry is *after* Dr. Clark (AD). The old Sherry is the one to be discarded, the one "...we don't want anymore," but the new Sherry is the one that is now created in the representative narcissistic image of Dr. Clark.

Sherry: "I'm just in pain and nothing can take the pain away."

Sherry is now holding her old glasses in her left hand. Angel leans into the camera and says, "Look at my hair today—ohhh…"

Sherry is looking at herself in the mirror with her new(self) glasses. The scene then cuts to Dr. Clark's resident supervisor, who appears periodically throughout the documentary.

Supervisor: "Did you give her the glasses?"

Dr. Clark: "I did."

Supervisor: "And?"

Dr. Clark: "They look good."

Supervisor: "Was she able to be happy?"

Dr. Clark: Frustrated snicker… "Not really."

Supervisor: "What did she say?"

Dr. Clark: "It was a brief moment that she truly enjoyed the new glasses."

Supervisor: "Did she say that she doesn't deserve them—on some level?"

Dr. Clark: "No, but I think she felt that way, because she expressed a lot of guilty feelings, right after I gave them to her."

Supervisor: "That's great that you did that… good." Then the supervisor smiles to the camera and walks away.

As is represented in the documentary, there appears to be a countertranferential dynamic between Dr. Clark and the supervisor that mutually supports not only their collective narcissism but also their collaborative naiveté.

One of the most critical aspects involved in the education and training of a psychotherapist, regardless of the academic discipline, is immersing oneself in their own therapy. Not just when a crisis emerges and more support is needed to traverse tumultuous psychic head waters, but rather an *ongoing* psychotherapeutic experience. Psychoanalysis, much to its collective credit, still requires being in analysis to be qualified as an analyst. However, virtually no other therapeutic paradigm demands the same of its clinical progeny.

It is not uncommon for one to attend a 'weekend training workshop' and thus declare themselves whatever that kind of therapist the workshop has purported to produce. There are those clinical *techniques* that require at each 'level' of training that the participant's sign a nondisclosure agreement with regard to what techniques will be taught. The more we emphasize one size fits all techniques and 'evidence-based' therapeutic paradigms the more we deemphasize the necessity of first and foremost working on ourselves as therapists.

No one comes into this world clean and no one goes out clean. However, it is essential that we take the precautions that we can to reduce or be aware of our own madness, projections, fantasized expectations and countless other prejudices as they emerge within the psychotherapeutic context. Not only does the patient stand a better chance of getting better treatment but we also, as clinicians, further enhance our own professional and personal growth.

Part III

Projective Identification and Serial Murder
(The Missing Link)

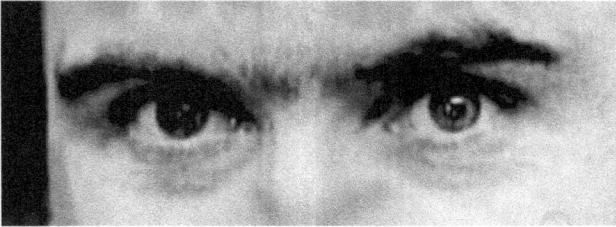

Part III
Projective Identification and Serial Murder
(The Missing Link)

The story is told of an automaton constructed in such a way that it could play a winning game of chess, answering each move of an opponent with a winning countermove. A puppet in Turkish attire and with a hookah in its mouth before a chessboard was placed on a large table. A system of mirrors created the illusion that this table was transparent from all sides. Actually a little hunchback who was an expert chess player sat inside and guided the puppet's hand by means of strings. One can imagine a philosophical counterpart to this device. The puppet called "historical materialism" is to win all the time. It can easily be a match for anyone if it enlists the service of theology, which today, as we know, is wizened and has to keep out of sight. [1940, Walter Benjamin "Theses on the Philosophy of History"]

To fascinate or charm somebody utterly keeps that person in check and gets them to act against their best interests for the interests of a few. [2009, John Espy]

Introduction

"It really wasn't hard you've got to understand I could just look at them and know they were my type you know what I mean? I was only wrong that one time in Oklahoma and I had a head cold. I treated the bitch real nice too, just tried to treat her real good and she fucked me by jumping out of my car running around like some kind of crazy bitch and then some fucking jerk drives around the curve and she jumps in the car with him … go figure. You want me to show you where the others are." [Ted Bundy to the author, Death Row, Florida State Penitentiary, 1988, one month before his execution.]

Take note that Bundy's statement ended with a *period*, even though from the content, it appears as though it should end with a *question mark*. However, if you reread Bundy's statement without putting the affective inflection of an interrogative at the end of his statement you will begin the process of understanding the projective identification process of the serial killer.

In this chapter, we will explore the psychostructural primitiveness of the serial murderer through the lens of projective identification. We will also examine the process of projective identification as the primary psychodynamic process that the serial killer uses to troll for his victims and lure them into his web of malignant projections. For the serial killer, perversion is the primary and *only* occupation of his life.

The unconscious and preconscious typography of the serial killer will also be delineated. This work is born out of more than thirty years of research, clinical interviews, and case consultations with convicted serial killers Ted Bundy, Jeffrey Dahmer, John Wayne Gacy, Edmund Kemper, Ottis Toole, Charles Pierce, Edward Gein, Richard

Ramirez, Donald Henry (Pee Wee) Gaskins and convicted serial kidnapper, pedophile, and likely serial killer Nathaneal Bar Jonah (who was also charged with the murder of a young man, Zachary Ramsay, however the charges were dropped). This essay represents one of the most comprehensive explorations of the psychostructural dynamics of the serial murderer. It is understood for our purposes that these individuals represent one of the most primitive forms of psychological expression of the human species

Childhood Trauma

Many of the childhood histories of serial killers are replete with *verifiable* horrors of childhood abuse flung far beyond what most normal individuals can begin to imagine. We see horrendous physical and sexual abuse intertwined with relentless bizarre psychological torment.

For example, at the age of five, Eddie Gein was chained naked, upside down, from a barn rafter by his father who then beat him with a shepherd's crook. Gein's father confessed to the family minister that he also penetrated his son's rectum with the crook in an attempt to purge Gein's soul from the evil his mother said that he was filled with. While his father was penetrating his rectum, Gein's mother would sit on a nearby hay bale screaming Bible verses, trying to "drive the Devil out of the boy." Gein died at Waupun State Prison in Wisconsin in 1984. His tortured life and the nightmares that he created for his victims was the spur for the movie *The Texas Chainsaw Massacre*. Obviously countless children suffer at the hands of sadistic parents and do not become serial killers. However, the broad lines of demarcation consistently fall into seven primary categories:

1. The age the abuse begins.

2. A maternal relationship that has not promoted separation but punished it severely or equated separation to psychic annihilation.

3. The intensity of the abuse, including psychological/physical torture combined with ongoing emasculation.

4. A *bizarre* element attached to the consistency of the abuse.

5. At what juncture(s) the developmental breach occurs.

6. The relationship of the victim to the abuser.

7. A history of traumatic brain injury—creating a hypofrontality, thereby impinging the mediation abilities of the frontal cortex and severely damaging the insula, which controls one's ability to identify and experience disgust.

As children, serial killers report engaging in acts of coprophilia, enuresis, fire setting, and cruelty and experimentation on animals. This typically begins with cruelty to their stuffed animals. These children also become involved in acts of psychological and physical malice to vulnerable children that goes considerably beyond the bounds of typical childhood aggression. Their internal representational worlds are constructed out of bizarre fantasies that include dreams and fantasies of dismemberment and murder as well as deep narcissistic and savior themes. It is not uncommon for these children to be very vocal about these fantasies to other children. Their behaviors set them apart from their childhood peers, frequently resulting in social isolation. Other parents in the neighborhood will commonly refer to them as an "odd" or "a strange little boy."

Jeffrey Dahmer acknowledged that he began eating his feces "right before I began school, about five or six, I guess. I liked the taste," he would say without *any* sense of disgust. Dahmer's mother, Joyce Flint, when interviewed by the author, stated that she observed Jeffrey at a young age sitting on the family porch, ripping the abdomen of his teddy bear open and attempting to eat its stuffing. As Dahmer got older, she said he progressed to small rodents, cats, dogs and at age seventeen, people. Flint referred to her son as a monster.

Frequently, for children with this kind of profile, lying and denial is the primary behavior they intersubjectively use to relate to the world. Theirs is not a necessity to tell the truth. Rather, they relate through perceptual distortions and possess an inability to modify either their beliefs or their perceptions. The most recent espial is that serial killers *do not* experience "disgust." For example, when one imagines eating feces, it brings about a visceral reaction of disgust. In individuals who lack the ability to experience disgust, there is minimal or no reaction to having such a thought or in having such an image presented to them. It is likely this revelation could result in the development of evaluative instruments to measure disgust and then to examine other behavioral and clinical markers to begin the process of early detection of these patterns.

The most recent individual involved in this study is Nathaneal Benjamin Levi Bar Jonah. Bar Jonah was convicted in May 2002 for sexual assault and kidnapping of three young boys in Great Falls, Montana. He was sentenced to one hundred thirty years without the possibility of parole. In October 2002, he was facing deliberate homicide charges for the murder of a ten-year-old boy, Zachary Ramsay. He was also accused of cooking, cannibalizing, and clandestinely feeding part of the child's remains to his neighbors in a spaghetti sauce. In an intriguing turn of events, the murder charges against Bar Jonah were abruptly dropped after the missing child's mother, Rachel Howard, agreed to testify for Bar Jonah. Howard stated that she believed that Bar Jonah "is innocent" and couldn't possibly "have had anything to do with my son's disappearance." The child's mother agreed to testify only after she and Bar Jonah exchanged letters over a two-year period while Bar Jonah was awaiting trial for the murder of her son. The night before the murder trial was going to commence, one of the prosecutors in the case walked into a restaurant and observed Bar Jonah's defense team having dinner with Howard. The murder charges were dismissed the following day. During the interviews conducted with this author, Bar Jonah stated, "Zach's mother *is* going to testify for me. We have been writing to each other for a long time and she is going to testify for me because there is *no* body. I've kept a close eye on her over these past few years. She'll do whatever I tell her to do." This statement of Bar Jonah's goes to the heart of this investigation.

What the Serial Killer is Seeking

Many essays have been written offering insights into the psycho-structural dynamics of the serial killer. Recently psychoanalyst Christopher Bollas (*Cracking Up*, 1995) pronounced that the serial killer was the "designated cultural representation of evil." Bollas's argument has some salient points. However, Bollas, like many other speculators, falls short in one significant area: he never interviewed any serial killers in formulating his assertions. Those that have, like the popular author, retired FBI agent John Douglas, frequently lack the clinical training to be able to delineate the deeply primitive psychological world in which the serial killer lives. Others take an exclusively behavioral approach, attempting to associate the behavior with reductionistic motives.

Motivations

The serial killer is not seeking to engage with his intended prey as a discrete human being. Rather, he is attempting to fuse with his intended victims, as one might envision two droplets of water merging together and becoming one. He accomplishes this through the process of projective identification.

The concept of projective identification was originally conceptualized by the British psychoanalyst Melanie Klein. Wilfred Bion further expanded the understanding of projective identification. We read much about the unconscious (Ucs) which is typically understood to be repressed psychic material. However, the astute reader will discover that Freud spoke of two Ucs: the repressed and the non-repressed; little has been written about the non-repressed Ucs. Yet the foundation of psychoanalysis rests on the theoretical premise of the *repressed* Ucs, which has become synonymous with the concept of Freudian conflict. Freud's theory of repression as a clinical entity focuses on a reemergence of repressed material. Repressed ideas return via psychic by-products that bypass the expurgated aspects of the mind. In treatment, the therapist listens or attunes to these censored aspects and over time a characterological pattern is revealed. Freud also proposed another theory of Ucs expression, one that does not center on the more esoteric and cryptic moments when a derivative suddenly appears out of the surfeit of relational associations. However, Freud's secondary theory of the Ucs suggests that implicit in the sequence of our thinking process is a chronoscopic logic. If we listen to the abrupt ideas that are presented to us as many lines of Ucs thought, there will be revealed a calculus that is discernible and represents a window to an individual's non-repressed inner psychic representations, a logic of a chronicle of representations. These non-repressed Ucs derivatives are important distinctions as we deconstruct the psyche of the serial killer. As we know, one of the difficulties that individuals with severe personality disorders experience is an inability to repress traumatic events, associations, or circumstances that produce psychic conflict. If one cannot repress, then the non-repressed psychic material must constantly compete in both waking and sleeping states for representation in its various forms. Therefore, projective identification is used psychically as an alternative to repression. This process is consistently replicated over and over again in the primitive psychic schema of the serial killer.

Projective Identification: A Psychic Calculus

Projective identification by definition is the process of consciously[3] or unconsciously interlacing affectively charged psychic residue (introjects of a malignant nature) and their accompanying behaviors (without their associated memories) with counter-resonating introjectively identified psychic material that already exists in the intended victim. In other words, projective identification is the implanting of emotionally charged psychological residue into another introjectively *fertile* person, or whose *own* counter-resonating introjective residue already exists within them. Specifically, victims who have survived encounters with serial killers describe experiencing a feeling of "just being taken over," "not being able to resist," "All of a sudden I lost my sense of who I was." Referring to the victims as *host* will now more precisely describe the parasitic mental organization of the serial killer. The serial killer's mental organization is devoid of *any* nonmalignant empathic concern for the life of another. The serial killer's bleak psychological world is one that seeks to devour the inner life of his prey.

In 2002, Bar Jonah said, "Things got a lot better for me in here [prison] when the guards and the other inmates began thinking and acting like I want them to. Now it's real good, well not real good, I take things one person at a time … you know." Even in this direct quote, Bar Jonah uses the "… *you know*," as an attempt to create a familiarity and projective collusiveness.

When Bar Jonah was ten years old, he and his friend "Kevin" were walking through the woods when eight older boys accosted them. "They hung Kevin between two trees and threw matches on him and set him on fire. They had me held down and pushed a tree branch all the way up my butt and made me suck them off while they tried to kill Kevin. I knew I had to save Kevin's life, so I fought them off and pulled the broom handle out of my butt and beat the boys up and cut Kevin down and saved his life." Factually, the type of assault Bar Jonah described would have resulted in severe rectal and anal tears. Kevin would have had obvious burns on his body. These types of injuries are not something that would go unnoticed by either boy's parents and would require emergency medical attention. Bar Jonah's mother, however, said she first heard about Bar Jonah's recollection, "about one year after he was sent to prison." She also said, "He *never* had *anything* like that happen to him. It just didn't *happen!*" Bar Jonah related the alleged event over and over again for the next twenty years and said it was "life changing." It appears that Bar Jonah hijacked the tale of being a heroized-victim from Wayne Chapman, convicted serial pedophile and alleged murderer. It was discovered that Bar Jonah opportunistically began using this story after Kevin was killed in an automobile crash.

The Process

When targeted hosts come in contact with a serial killer, they become enveloped in the labyrinth of the killer's malignant projections. Victims who have survived attacks report experiencing an abrupt psychological disorientation as the serial killer's malignant psychic larvae are deposited into their psyche. However, even though the affect deposited into the host is introjectively resonant, it is nonetheless a *not-theirs* affect. In other words, it belongs to the killer and not to the host. The not-theirs affect is now residing within the host, without an accompanying memory associated with the affect. This typically results in the host beginning to dissociate or experience a state of unrealness. Depending upon the voraciousness of the malignant introject this can be experienced as a sudden psychic shock to the host's mental life. The host now begins to experience what has been described as a "state of perplexity"[2] created by the contradictory absence of an associated memory with the deposited affect.

In essence, this is a seizing of psychic control of the host. This dynamic psychologically "short-circuits" and then resets the host's self by charging the introjects of the host with the serial killer's now resonant malignant projective residue.

Memory and Affect

It is important to briefly discuss memory and its associated affect. Each memory template that we maintain neurologically has an associated affective tag. These associative templates are believed to be resident in the cerebellum. With each template, we remember what might be best described as moments, not days. For example, in recalling the template of a particularly pleasant sexual encounter, we also experience a semblance of the affects associated with that encounter, which may result in a physiological response of arousal. When we recall the death of a loved one, the remembrance is flooded with not just memories but also with feelings of pain and loss. The constellations of our recollections are composed of *analogous* memories and affects. If, however, an affect ascends without an associated memory, psychic confusion ensues. If the affect is experienced without the memory, it results in a sense of perplexity and, depending upon the intensity of the affect, can devolve into psychic chaos. The more intense the affect, the greater the potential for ensuing psychic mayhem.

During the interplay between the serial killer and the host, there is a dynamic shift from an intrapsychic process to an interpsychic process. The ego of the host becomes overwhelmed by the serial killer's projective identification so that it can no longer carry out its primary function: that being the moment-to-moment mental management of the host's intrapsychic world. The extreme malignant nature of the serial killer's projective identification results in a psychic exsanguination of the host's ego, which in essence then becomes anemic. This underscores the co-defense of denial in the serial killer, which serves as the plinth for projective identification. The denial creates a quasi-sheltered psychological space that permits the serial killer to deceive himself into believing that once the psychically intolerable material is projected into the host, it will begin to lose its domination over the serial killer. The denial acts as a psychological veneer that permits the deranged illusions to colonize the recesses of the killer's mind. This allocates for the killer a period of refraction or a psychic hiatus, from the supremacy of the self-annihilating aggression associated with the malignancy of the introjective material that the killer is projecting.

The period of time associated with the refractorial repose is directly proportional to the potency of the introjective material. As the affect becomes more concentrated it begins to gain momentum as it ascends. Affect for the serial killer can only be contained through denial and projective identification and then only for a short period of time. As the serial killer projects the affect into the host, it neurophysiologically triggers the release of a serotonin bath, which is soothing to the killer as it is released into his cerebral circulatory system. However, the serial killer has not rid himself of the tormenting introjects. Rather, what he has projected are introjective fragments or in other words introjective waste material. This is the equivalent of psychic elimination. The ascension of the malignant introjects is similar to a psychological peristalsis. Although a crude metaphor, if relief is not forthcoming, the serial killer experiences a panic, not unlike experiencing bowel rumblings with limited if any opportunities for expulsion. Hence, the host becomes the psychological toilet via the parasitic nature of the projections.

One of the problems for the killer lies within the dynamics of the intensity of the reverie associated with the denial. Through its denial, the serial killer believes that once the introjective psychic residue is projected, it will no longer stalk and haunt him from within. Ironically, the psychic waste shed by the introjects through projective identification actually allows for a revitalization of the malignant introjects that even further consumes the intrapsychic world of the serial killer. The malignant introject uses projective identification as an unconscious means of psychic replication and rejuvenation.

This is an important factor in how character pathology psychically devours the ego structure over time and becomes an intractable and self-annihilating psychic state. This course of self-annihilation is tantamount to a state of psychological terminality. Through the projective identification process, the affect fragments associated with the excruciating psychic material no longer reside within the serial murderer but are now interlaced into the introjective fabric of his prey. A surrogate form is now sustaining these intolerable affect fragments. Therefore the ascension of the threatening affect in the serial killer has been temporarily defused and is no longer experienced as acutely ominous. The threat has now intrapsychically rescinded and the killer's affected psychic status is restored. However, the intrapsychic threat has now been replaced by an interpsychic threat.

The etiology of this process evolves from several interrelated interpersonal dynamics:

As the mother's fragile intrapsychic status begins fragmenting, the child's subjective experiences become increasingly more definable. In order for the mother to maintain her intrapsychic homeostasis, the maternal empathy is replaced by projective identification of a bizarre and incoherent autobiographical narrative. It is infeasible for the maternal form1 to be able to imagine that the child has a subjective experience that does not involve the mother without creating an intrapsychic inferno. Therefore, the child becomes an unwitting actor on this bizarre stage of the maternal narrative. In this scenario, there is never any possibility for psychic extrication. One example of this fusion is observing the mother carefully scanning the room, looking to see if she is being looked at as she publicly complains about her child whom she is training to act out so she can exercise her exhibitionism.

These dynamics set in motion a deprivation of the child's ability to be able to achieve the basic developmental foundations necessary for the emergence of a viable differentiated self. The lack of the mother's ability to permit and nourish individuation creates a warping of what we typically would describe as the mirroring function. Therefore, the psychological encoding of the infant's iconographic world is malformed and distorted. This is impelled by unrelenting anxiety that is born out of a mystification and bewilderment of the representational conflict that exists between the inner and outer world. Imagine for a moment a distorted carnival fun house mirror.

The silver coating is weather worn. The mirror is battered and bruised from being hauled from town to town. One stands in front of the mirror seeking, with increasing agitation and desperation, a recognizable perceptual echo. The vermiculated shape takes distinguishable objects and skews their perception. Glinnwater (personal communication, November 2008) has suggested the mirroring function is not just one of reflection but also one of absorption. This important observation takes into consideration the serial killer's fractured ego. Therefore, not only does the ascension of anxiety usurp what minimal ego function the serial killer possesses but now he experiences another artery of encroaching anxiety at the possibility of a complete loss of control through being absorbed by the host that he attempts to consume through projective identification.

As the strange life of the serial killer continues to devolve over time, he seeks alternate forms to contain and clarify his representational experiences that now pulsate within his deeply disturbed mental life. The labyrinth of this increasingly indecipherable representational world, growing steadily into a continually threatening hydra, stupefies the serial killer. Clinically we see a child whose mirroring through the reflective lens of the mother is warped by primordial, cannibalistic self-consuming similes that continuously threaten the killer with psychic annihilation. This dynamic creates an ominous difficulty in the killer's ability to discriminate reality from fantasy and the actual from the amorphous. Ultimately this leads to an isolated concretized, patternistic, and restrictive affective life. His collective world is wholly objectified (exploitive/manipulative/psychopathic) rather than subjectified (differentiated and communicative). Affect within this type of psychostructural lexicon becomes contaminated and unreliable with regards to its accurateness to all representational associations. This is a strategic psychic determiner in how the serial killer manages the ascension of these enigmatic affects; through physical aggression against his own body (retroflected) or in relation to others (projected/projective identification).

No more than the killer's mother could imagine her son's individuated subjective experience, the serial killer cannot imagine possessing the psychological assets that others have acquired who have successfully negotiated their developmental milestones and not been subjected to a lifetime of torture by a cadre of malignant introjects. The killer's lack of competence to contain the ascension of affect compels him to experience all aspects of his bizarre internal world externally and through the fantasized unblemished objectification of the other.

The question has arisen many times in the literature asking what the serial killer is seeking when he is trolling for prey and how he is able to so readily identify his intended victims. The answer to this question is that the killer is trolling for *projections* from the potential host. These projections serve as markers for successful introjective resonance. It is a mere inconvenience to the serial killer that humans happen to be attached to these projections. The serial killer is trolling for a host that either psychologically or behaviorally manifests the specific vulnerabilities of the host's introjective structure through the projections the host portrays. In other words, the killer is able to detect a potential victim's susceptibility by acutely observing his behavioral and affective tells. This allows him to be able to discriminate which potential prey will give him the greatest liberation (refractory period) for the longest period of time. In essence, the best psychological bang for his buck. When the serial killer encounters a potential introjective heir in a social setting, he begins to preview them as possible future prey. For example, Ted Bundy actively trolled for hosts when he went to political functions in Washington state. He would ask a standard series of questions as part of his previewing process. Consistently he would set up the same "What if" game. Seductively, Bundy would boyishly say, "Hey, let's you and I play a game. What would you do if we just started dating and I broke my leg?" From her response, Bundy would ascertain the susceptibility of the potential host. If she stated, "Oh ... [laden with affective seduction], I would take care of you and nurse you back to health," Bundy would then determine that she desired to be consumed by him and that he had, in this brief momentary exchange, been able to engage this young woman's introjective vulnerabilities. His initial attempts at engaging her as a potential host through projective identification would have proven to be successful. Bundy would then move on to what he referred to as another "candidate" who he would screen in a similar fashion. "I would interview each candidate until I found the one who desired to offer me the most assistance in my quest."

This is also a prime example of the process of excorporation. Excorporation is the psychic space that lies in between the individual engaging in projective identification and the potential host. It is the enhancement and eventual closing of this psychic space by the killer that serves as the affective conduit by which the killer's malignant empathy can enter and seat in the host. Excorporation serves as the interpsychic bridge that permits the transfer of psychic material via projective identification. It is important not to lose sight of the fact that serial killers, without exception, view *everyone* as potential prey. He is incapable of experiencing, much less manifesting, nonexploitive empathy. Empathy expressed at this level of primitiveness is manifested for only one reason, to entice intended prey into exposing their introjective vulnerabilities through projection so as to become an unwitting participant in their own quasi-voluntary demise.

The psychostructural configuration of the serial killer rivals reptilian indifference in its primitiveness. As part of this process, the killer will frequently select his prey months before they are actually taken. Bundy, for example, told of an incident where he met a young woman at a political fundraiser. "She was perfect, absolutely perfect for me, everything about her cried I am you and you are me and we *will* be together. Ha Ha Ha Ha." He further stated that, "The time just wasn't right, you know, I wasn't hungry, I wasn't in need. But I watched her for about three months, kept an eye on her and when I felt the hunger we became one. It was blissful." During his trial Richard Ramirez sat at the defense table and wrote poetry. Ramirez wrote the following poem while delivering enticing glances to a particular female juror:

> *I am the consumer of souls*
> *destroyer of their dreams*
> *The nightmares which I incur*
> *wake you with your screams.*

I am the end of your innocence
the planting of my fears and tears
I eat away the inside of your mind
and kill you with my fears.
I am the words you cannot speak
and the acts you don't
know why you do
I am the twisted childhood memories
that you cannot remember
The terror in your voice
as painfully you plea to me through you
To fight the urges inside of you
to end up becoming just like me.

Several weeks after he was sentenced for murder, the juror *fell in love* with Ramirez and petitioned through three different attorneys a plea for his release so they could be married. In the petitioning documents to the court the juror stated that she had "never felt so loved." Later this young woman also stated that, "It felt like it was just Richard and me in the courtroom, just the two of us like we were able to touch each other, I don't know what happened, I felt like I lost my mind." In her statement, the juror's use of "Richard" is representative of her familiarity with Ramirez and is another example of how the projective identification was manifest.

Once the serial killer makes his selection he experiences a brief refractory period. He has made his choice, the initial anxiety is quelled, and he is able to concentrate his efforts now on capturing his prey. Physically capturing the host is typically the least disturbing aspect to the pursuit.

After the initial anxiety is dissipated, the serial killer typically experiences a shock wave of anxiety. Successive and rapid ascensions of pulses of intense anxiety are now experienced, due to the fact that he is now beginning to project his introjective material into his host.

At this stage in the sequential projective-introjective interplay, the serial killer begins to feel abandoned by the harsh and critical introjects that he is projecting into the host. A resolve of how to manage the host, who is now in possession of the serial killer's projected introjected psychic material, must rapidly be made. The level of psychic threat the killer experiences, now being out of possession of the introjective waste, is proportional to how severe and threatening the affective material is that now resides within the introjective host.

It is at this point that the host is at the most acutely vulnerable state. The killer must now solve the dilemma of what to do with the projected material that is now being maintained on life-support by the host. Unfortunately for the host the verdict consistently rendered includes torture and death. The serial killer not only wishes to rid himself of the intolerable psychic material, he is also attempting to enhance his *affectedness* or affective neutrality, with a sense of mastery and control over the deposited projections. He then attempts to punish, maim, and annihilate the disturbing projections through horrendous and heinous acts directed against the host. In addition, the killer also has to be concerned with the fact that once the projective identification of the malignant introjects is complete, he is likely to be consumed with transitory psychotic paranoia of an external attack because of the aggression associated with the introjects now residing outside of himself. The process being described is not episodic. Rather it is one that is representative of the fundamental nature of the killer. Everything he knows himself to be and how he exists in the world is compelled by the previously described psychodynamic process taking one form or another.

As the affect associated with the malignant introjects begins re-ascending, the killer's *affected* psychic state is now being threatened. The cycle now begins anew. The malignant introjects are emitting recharged aggression that is experienced by the killer as even more vicious and ominous as the length of the refractory period degrades over time. The time span of the cycle is not determined by moon phases or other popularized notions.

Rather it is determined by three interrelated factors:

1. The amount of psychic reprieve the killer obtains from the implantation and elimination of the malignant introjective waste.

2. The time period associated for the revitalization of the malignant introjects.

3. The intensity and concentration of the associated anxiety and intrapsychic threat produced by the revitalization process.

Exposure to violent developmentally derailing traumatization also plays a significant role in the psychogenesis of the expression of bizarre violent behavior. Most subjective experiences normally have a correlative template of stable relational associations. However, for the serial killer, the ever-shifting of intrapsychic tectonics is discontinuous, with the only continuity being the malignant introjections of the mother's projections. These projections are not just content laden but also contain the psychic DNA associated with the projections, including their affective components.

The serial killer has the intrapsychic experience of attempting to control the introjects of the maternal form, believing erroneously that the *external* representational world can be controlled *internally*. The individual whose psychostructural world is woven together in this manner attempts to rearrange the external world to map or correlate to his fantasized representational world. These are not projections per se but rather a superimposing of the typography of one set of representations onto another. These superimposed representations now more closely match or associate with the affect laden projections that bind together the templates contained within the orbit of the quasi-relationship between the killer and his host. These projections are then experienced introjectively as having a life of their own which demand satisfaction in the form of self-punishment or other acts of contrition that result in psychological annihilation over time. The serial killer is then cast into an intrapsychic vortex that requires not only ridding himself of the introjects but also to satisfy the demands of the introjects.

A coexisting psychostructural process also lives concurrently in individuals functioning at this level of psychic primitiveness. We have already established that the serial killer is under psychological siege from his inner world. Metaphorically this dynamic is similar to the biochemistry of reabsorption. When the body is suffering from extreme calcium deficiency it begins to feed on its own skeletal system.

In the serial killer, the profoundly harsh, critical, and self-murderous introjective structure is attacking the vulnerable infantile-self, which has no psychological resources by which to defend against such a consistent assault. The infantile-self is then projected via projective identification into an introjective host who then resonates with this aspect of the killer. The serial killer then must eradicate not only the harsh introjects but also the vulnerable self in order to purge the intrapsychic threat-cycle that contributes to him experiencing himself in a chronic state of threat. This dynamic is precisely the manner by which Ted Bundy was able to initially woo his victims into participating in his projective charades. In an almost cliché portrayal, Bundy "picked-up" young coeds by feigning injury to his arm, trumpeted himself bound in a plaster cast, seeking the most timid and passive female he could prey upon—being assured of her necessary responsiveness (discovered through previewing) to his contrived vulnerability. The victim resonated with the projection of his vulnerable self and then found herself stunned by the sudden materialization of the punitive, terrorizing introject which manifested through a transformation of Bundy's facade.

Although the focus of our discussion is limited to serial killers it must also be stated that we see *similar* psychological dynamics manifested by men who batter as well as who engage in other aggressive or violent acting-out behaviors, particularly those involved in aggressive acts toward those more vulnerable than the assailant. However, the central question that must be addressed with regard to this factor is, why do some individuals become serial murderers while others do not?

In order to adequately respond to this question we must be able to envision the inner world of the serial killer. We must move beyond our countertransferential abhorrence or voyeuristic fascination and mine deeply into our own demons to discover how these individuals come to be the way they are. When a biochemist seeks to conceptualize a chemical structure, he cannot do so without understanding the structure from the molecular level. The same is true for the psychological aspects of human development. One of the lowest common denominators with regard to pathological character development is the serial killer. Yet many argue that others are exposed to horrible and terrible abandonment and abuse and do not evolve into serial murderers and of course on the surface this is a statement of fact. However, one of the critical aspects of this argument is the multigenerational dynamic that accompanies the psychological and social history of serial killers. The dynamics we have described must also be recognized from a social gene standpoint, which represents a series of intergenerational psychological mutations. The serial killer is not a case of a "good boy gone bad." Rather he is an individual that has been selected to be the psychological repository of generation after generation of abandonment and rage and to possess no identity of his own. Through the projective identification process the killer is ultimately seeking an identity through evacuation of not only the mother's harsh and critical introjects but also of intergenerational psychopathology.

For example, during an interview with Ed Gein, at Mendota Mental Health Institute, he said, "I wus diggin that hole in the cemetery and got down to the box with *it* in it and gettin the box open wus real real hard, you ever try to get a box open while it's in the ground, it's real hard you have to be real strong to do that. Then I take my jack knife and take *it* apart you know not all the parts just what I needed, ain't lots who know this but you know you take their pussy you know and put it down in some underwear and then you can wear it you know. If you get one of those pussies that's big and floppy you can almost pull it right over your head like a t-shirt. I never did find one with enough stretchy. I kept lookin til they got me though. You know how long titties last? If you dip um just right in formaldehyde you can put um on ya chest and make um fit just right, ya know." The act that Gein was relating was horrific; however, Gein was not just killing for the sake of killing, nor was he attempting to resurrect his mother. Rather he was attempting to *create a* mother. He also psychotically imagined that by building a new mother from "spare parts" from the "bone yard" that he would be able to rebirth himself. Gein attempted to neutralize the Gehenna of the unrelenting malignant introjects.

Yet, at each of his bizarre junctures, he slowly came to realize the futility of his efforts to construct a mother in his own image. By reassembling his mother from spare parts collected from living hosts and corpses he exhumed from the cemetery, Gein imagined that he would be able to return his old mother's torrential viciousness to his new mother and awaken from the nightmare. Of course, Gein could not envision that he had become his mother's image. Should he have succeeded, he would have resurrected a profoundly revitalized constellation of malignant introjects, being of a magnitude that he could not begin to fathom. It was as though his mother was compelling him to resurrect her from the dead. In the end Gein said, "I wanted to give it all back to Momma but if I did I'da felt way too guilty, so I guess it's best that they got to me when they did. That way Momma and I didn't have to go through it all over again."

Postscript

Recently there have been developments in the area of neurobiology related to understanding disgust. In a series of experiments Italian neuroscientist Giacomo Rizzolatti has discovered that the brain's insula of Reil plays a key role in one's ability to experience disgust. Interestingly, if one thinks about the heinous acts that serial killers perpetrate on their victims, it would be impossible for them to be able to experience disgust. It is doubtful if readers of this article can imagine cutting off a corpse's labia in an attempt to reconstruct their mother or cannibalizing a young boy. However, in the examples of Eddie Gein and Nathan Bar Jonah, they could not have engaged in these behaviors were they able to experience disgust.

It is not atypical for serial killers to have come before the youth courts in their adolescence charged with crimes of animal torture or arson as well as assaults of vulnerable victims. They are usually given perfunctory and boilerplated psychological evaluations as part of their adjudication process. Comprehensive questions regarding disgust should be included and their reactions noted and discussed. The author is now working on a series of standardized questions to begin to ascertain an individual's range of responses to disgust and to formulate baselines. Standardized questions that would examine for disgust may be predictive with regard to the heinousness of a crime an individual might be prone to commit. Intelligence quotients will also need to be factored into the investigation. In certain cases, there will be a correlation to imaging studies relating to the perfusion status of the island of Reil as well as examining for hypofrontality.

Endnotes

1. "Form" is far more precise than the Kleinian "object." The term as well as the multitude of representations of "object" lends itself to a conceptualization that possesses some type of physical anatomy. Further, "object" implies a static quality which does not adequately represent intra – or inner psychic life, which is amorphous and osmotic with each psychic pulse.

2. "State of perplexity": This phrase was iterated to the author by several victims of serial killers who managed to survive or escape.

3. Formerly only thought to be an unconscious process; as the psychodynamics of projective identification becomes habituated over the life span of the individual the process of projective identification becomes increasingly recognized consciously. However, the recognition occurs in retrospect through an analysis of the behaviors that led to a specific outcome.

Distillations

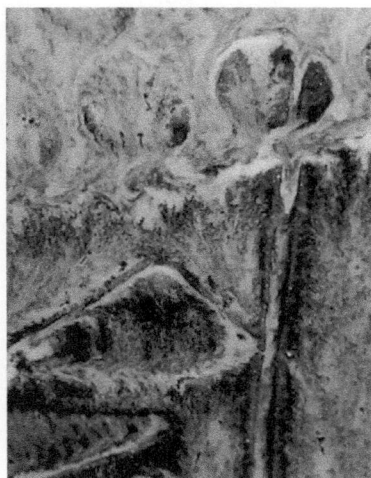

The Hard Road

This moment…frozen in time
as down the road I amble
A well-worn path whose trail I tread
An ambulance speeds by…
dry fall leaves scatter whirling and twirling
Beowulf cries mockingly,
"Beware, beware trails of
gray that promise to hold the way"

Down the seedy alleyway and out the sides of my eyes I capture
lurking faces, peering from chimney brick doorways
as on to Fagan's Hand Black Widow Fantasy Shop I wander
Hard rubber pricks, frigid plastic cunts
leather harnesses and steel-cock rings
A buck-toothed black bastard with a smoke shriveled face
smiles and tells me what I can't love without

A whore in the corner with
teeth as white as Mahjong blocks
pass delicately over an old man's cock
Lips wet and smooth try to soothe
the bitter taste of age

An ugly voyeur leers from his dark gloom
as sounds of a second stroking cock
fill the room

Stopped in for a coffee
A bottled blonde with a cocky rocking head
throws me the glance of her lazy eye open far too wide
snorts her greasy haired frenemy to death
through her flared upturned Pekinese nose
At a chrome legged yellow and white checkered table
a fawning once-muscled man
tries to impress a has-been
whose long thin cigarette

rides on her pale thick lips
Her once proud jelly breasts
buoy up to the rhythm of each restless breath
Pretending to be interested
in the boring fat man's
better than my brother's story
The pleasures of love found
far too late to undo the carnage of lust
"Goody-Goody" plays on the jute
coffee's cold, time to go

Shuffling down the road, an old man wearing a gravel-pocked face
cloaked in a Salvation Army Band hand-me down coat
walks through life in brown broken shoes and a shit-stained suit
Squared leathered hands with fingers thick as grubs
are brown and wrinkled with the scars of life
Cupping a blues harp he blows one tune alone
"Short time here, long time gone",
the lost will of a West Virginia Miner
A sunken widow of no one staggers by, the "Belle Heaulmiere"?
Two heads turn as though they're one
knowing eyes meet, knowing eyes sag
…a silent moment of untold sadness
A fancy sidewalk-scarred
cardboard case lays open and bare
begging silver tokens of
guilt-ridden sausage-dog walking passer bys
some stop to listen some stop to stare
My half-dollar spins end over end
as I slip away looking for my indifference
that, like a ghost, has suddenly turned into charity
A deaf and dumb beggar puffs up his fruit ripe cheeks
while cranking his hurdy-gurdy with his only good arm
The music box becalmed, the rosined wheel strikes no strings
The tin cup begging on his belt
stays quiet as I go on about my way
Captured by the floating scent of cotton candy

My nose turns high to the sky

The carnival has come to town

There bounding by
a round headed curlylocks
with wondrous blue eyes
and chubby chunky little hands
one clutching a yellow balloon in tow
the other settling the unruly folds of her pretty new dress
from the panting of the threatening storm
Her short fat legs with their thick little feet
in way too big saddle-shoes
kick dusty stones
The wind, now, so still…
God's son shines
The silence-snatching breeze
begins its twists through the canopies
How brief the moment
between discovery and loss
There to my left the Grand Inquisitor
rides astride a fine chestnut steed
with its sharpened cut nose and flowing mane
adorned is he in his fatherly robe
The blacked cowled holy man nods suspiciously
with his alert and dangerous eyes
when then as quick as thought he draws the sign of the cross
like a swordsman who stays dry in the rain
Behind my back the galloped ground quakes

A collapse-chested scalloped faced ectomorph
with dry cracked lips and Appalachian slivers
whose lucky-strike rolled-up sleeve
hardly hides tattoos of loves gone bye
makes the chipped-paint horseys
go around and around and around
Bringing the long arm switch down
the galloping stallions begin to slow with a *whoa*…

A red and white neckerchiefed
crimson haired little cow-poke
dismounts with a prideful plunk
The pony man's *mal de ojo* heats the eyes and
freezes the little pardner in his stride
As his grizzled tongue swipes the stubbly chin
over and over, again and again
The mouth that speaks
to no one mumbles
in a long raspy drawl,
"Hey there little cow-poke
if you ain't gonna be my pal
I'm gonna crack your skull"
The wavy strands stand end on end
as the whine of the pumping calliope
quickly loses its happy wind
A callused, gnarled nub flips a spit-wet butt
tumbling through the acrid air
that now lays smoldering on the road
The burnt-out end of a smoky day… so they say

Tears begin to fall; the air is rich with the smell
of cold water on hot concrete, sounds of pawed thawed acorns
as black squirrels watch me from the forest

A distant clap of thunder heavy with lightmares
shows me the way

As I lay sleeping a bomber passes overhead
My dreams tremble…

Chock Full Of Nuts

Rocking to and fro lost in her madness
rolling her head from side to side
atop her warm doughy body
with thick legs that from behind
look like water logged tree trunks

"Will you still love me tomorrow"
plays loudly on the radio that she
clutches to her one left breast
Her thick wooden movements make her
look like she is walking in stone cold molasses
as she sways out of time to an in time tune
"…Long long time ago I can still remember
a little girl with thin red hair…*la la la la la*"

Her glazed eyes roll to the sky
as a misty memory reaches for her
like a wet hand through a late night fog
Oh that sunny day with daddy e
clapping his happy hands and
acting surprised when he was not and
laughing and laughing and laughing and laughing
and then…without skipping a beat
swinging her high in the air with that sweet
curly red hair twirling…into magic pigtails
With only a daddy's daughter's pride
she sees the tear in his eye and
smells his smoky breath as he calls her name

Now a long time's gone by
and at least once a day
she sits around and thinks
about when she wasn't alone
For our own good she lives carefully locked away
patiently waiting for anyone to say "I still love you today"…

Forget me knots

Golden haired long faced
round headed little girl
Big blue (like the whale) sad eyes
ready to blow her brains out

Ice Breakers

Where so ever
could a love so precious
be found that rejoices
in the cold late night
echoes of the sound of cracking ice
breaking beneath its feet

Neggers

In the barbershop some yesterdays ago now
a red headed fat man extolled
the sanctity and intelligence of whites and
the impurity and ignorance of blacks
"Their jest dumb neggers I tell you,
we made the mistake by not sending them back to Afraka"

It is "nigger" I say, my one time curly hair falling into my lap
"You're spelling the word wrong as you say it"
My war hero barber, who served as a cook
at the front says, "uh huh, uh huh" but I don't know about what

"Don't tell me boy I grew up with neggers,
I know how stupid they are, you ain't goin
tell me nothing bout them I don't already know"

I nodded assuredly that he
was all the proof that was ever necessary
for the white man's superiority over the "negger"
He looks at me in brotherhood shaking his head up and down
"Yep I told you son, I know my neggers"

A Sister's Lament

What a disappointing day, Sister says
I couldn't find anything I wanted
at the hardware store and

I won't be able to kill the nuns

The last time I saw your face

My big house, the money's been good
Lots of this and lots of that
My bankers on the phone
my new best buddy
Wants more of my business
A Big man am I now

At my stained glass door
I hear the God–Damned beggar
Pound, Pound, Pounding, calling me

Through the key hole there he stands
the thick-yellow weathered skin, grizzled beard
and battered Bible clutched under his filthy pit
Doesn't he know who I am
He insults my self-importance…

I Jerk open the door and
he audaciously reaches for my hand
"Could I work for some food, Buddy"
The son-of-a-bitch, called me "Buddy"

Jesus Christ, How do you know who I am
"Get off my porch you lice infested bastard," I say
The old man's gaze then burns my soul
Yes Buddy, I know who you are, and now I
see you too know who I am,
as He turns walking forever away from me
I begin to weep…
As there, my last hope of salvation
vanishes in a distant fading light…

Smokes

As I strike my pen to paper

I ignite worlds my soul weeps to embrace

A Summer Soulstice

Tonight on this summer's soulstice
I look out over the eastern mountains
And thru the black storm clouds
arc two brilliant rainbows
Of course the reader, who we dare not
speak ill of, cries in aghast…
"My God, not another damn poem about a rainbow"
To which I reply "No, no dear reader,
I would not subject you to that"
This is a poem about my pending death
from a diagnosis I was just given that I did not want.
And, looking out through my windows
at the rainbows fading away
I merely wondered
how many more rainbows
I will live to see.
So you see dear reader,
the subject of this poem was not
a hooky grade school teacher's chore
But a mere comment on death's presence that
I feel against my back…

Vapors

A captured moment…
As you lay sleeping
knowing I exist lovingly
in the vapors of your dreams

With Heraclitis In Mind

A Hairyclittian on fire
with philosophical desire

Working Girl

There was a whore I knew
we never fucked but
once she tipped up her ass
and offered herself to me
Right after she raised her shirt
to show me the ruby red
scars the bullets had left on her chest
by the mark who wasn't pleased

Last Watch

Each night as I
close my eyes to sleep
I wonder, if there will
be a next and a next and a ...
How many nexts are left?

Great Poseidon, mythic water watcher and
puppeteer from afar calls forth
Hypnos to carry me through
my turbulent slumber
beyond Morpheus to the final isle
of Mors which simply... is no more

Acknowledgements

THIS BOOK COULD NOT have been written without the privilege of experiencing my patients' pain, losses, sorrows, and joy over these now many years of practice. I also have had the privilege of working with many extraordinary teachers and supervisors. Dr. Howard Haas Fink, my therapist, supervisor and friend of more than thirty years, left his lasting influence as to how I see and interact with the world. Much of the material presented in this book was presented to Dr. Fink over the course of our work together. R. D. Laing, who was my supervisor for many years, remained true to his dedication in seeing beyond illusions and in helping me to more fully comprehend the *nature* of projective-identification. Sheldon Kopp, with whom I conducted a supervision group, also provided profoundly important insights about navigating through life's inevitable pain as well as letting oneself embrace joy. Twenty-five years of working with Isadore From emphasized the great importance of the specifics of language and integrity in the clinical setting. I salute Harold Searles, for having been so self-revealing and comfortable with his own craziness. "Thank you" to my friend, photographer Ralph Gibson who has been immensely supportive of my photographic endeavors over the years. Members of the American Academy of Psychotherapists provided much love and support early on in my career. *Clinical Dicta and Contra Dicta* could not have been written without the love of my wife, psychotherapist Treasa Glinnwater, to whom this book is dedicated. Please note that all of the material in this book are composites of different individuals and situations and do not represent any one individual or set of circumstances.